Pastor Tommy Barnett takes our poetic term "walk of faith" into unbelievable, literal and thrilling dimensions. You will journey with him into a mind and heart odyssey as big as the whole wide world. You will want to explode out of your little world to do exploits for God you never dreamed possible. This is must reading for anyone, young or old, who wants God's best in life.

—PAUL CROUCH, FOUNDER AND PRESIDENT
TRINITY BROADCASTING NETWORK

My warm friend and fellow preacher of the gospel has detailed in *Adventure Yourself* the stirring account of hearing God's voice to launch forth on impossible ventures (that most would run from) and "trying the spirits," until he feels this is what God wants him to do. His book excites me, makes me laugh and cry and enables me to see that God is determined to use the Tommy Barnetts to reach the unreachable before Jesus returns. I say, "Read this book!"

—ORAL ROBERTS, FOUNDER AND CHANCELLOR
ORAL ROBERTS UNIVERSITY

Your adventure will begin by reading this remarkable book. Thank You, God, for Tommy Barnett!

—DYAN CANNON
ACTRESS

Whether fulfilling his dreams through the ministry of the Dream Center in Los Angeles, California, or sharing his dream with thousands of others through the hundreds of ministries in Phoenix, Arizona, Tommy Barnett believes that living the Christian life is the greatest adventure of all time. Now *Adventure Yourself* will show you how to live the Christian life the way God intended it to be lived.

—DR. PAT ROBERTSON
CHAIRMAN OF THE BOARD AND CEO
THE CHRISTIAN BROADCASTING NETWORK

Knowing and following Jesus is meant to be the greatest pleasure in life. In *Adventure Yourself,* Tommy Barnett beckons Christians to step out of their comfort zones, to take up their crosses and to follow Jesus in making a difference in their world. This book will help believers live fuller, more meaningful lives!

—BILL MCCARTNEY
FOUNDER AND PRESIDENT, PROMISE KEEPERS

Adventure

Yourself

Tommy Barnett

CREATION
H O U S E

ADVENTURE YOURSELF by Tommy Barnett
Published by Creation House
A division of Strang Communications Company
600 Rinehart Road
Lake Mary, FL 32746
www.creationhouse.com

Unless otherwise noted, all Scripture quotations are from
the New King James Version of the Bible. Copyright ©
1979, 1980, 1982 by Thomas Nelson, Inc., publishers.
Used by permission.

Scripture quotations marked KJV are from the King James
Version of the Bible.

Scripture quotations marked NIV are from the Holy Bible,
New International Version. Copyright © 1973, 1978,
1984, International Bible Society. Used by permission.

Scripture quotations marked NRSV are from the New
Revised Standard Version of the Bible. Copyright © 1989
by the Division of Christian Education of the National
Council of the Churches of Christ in the USA. Used by
permission.

Library of Congress Cataloging-in-Publication Data:

Barnett, Tommy.
   Adventure yourself / by Tommy Barnett.
      p. cm.
   ISBN 0-88419-665-8
   1. Christian life. 2. Barnett, Tommy. I. Title.

BV4501.2. B38287 2000
248.4–dc21

                        99-58697
                        CIP

0 1 2 3 4 5 6 vp 7 6 5 4 3 2 1
Printed in the United States of America

I am excited to dedicate this book to my only daughter, Kristie! Her lifelong dream has been to be a great mother and wife, and she is accomplishing that great adventure with the zeal and love for life that are her trademarks.

Kristie is a great adventurer, and makes every day an exciting adventure. As her father, loving her is one of my great joys in life—and one of my greatest adventures because she is so easy to love. She is much more than a loving daughter—she is my buddy and friend.

Kristie, this book is dedicated to you, a great adventurer who brings great joy not only to her father and family, but to everyone you come into contact with. God bless you. I love you and thank God for you.

Contents

ADVENTURE YOURSELF

Foreword

THERE IS NO one more qualified to encourage us to adventure ourselves than Pastor Tommy Barnett. He knows of what he speaks, for truly his life and ministry exemplify a consistent series of adventures.

Eleven members of this pastoral staff team at Phoenix First Assembly have been here for at least ten years—we know of no other church staff in America that can say that. We love the adventurous path we're on, and like Pastor Barnett, we attempt to wring every drop out of every day in this most exciting adventure of the ministry of the gospel of the Lord Jesus Christ. Pastor Barnett has taught us to make every day a masterpiece, to go out to find needs and fill them, to prepare our hearts to maximize the moment-by-moment experiences so that we can fully adventure into abundant living.

Even the most expert and daring mountain climbers, when adventuring through the Himalayas of Tibet, seek out the native Sherpa guides—because they live there! Those guides know the shortcuts, the most beautiful venues, and they have seen the pitfalls and potential avalanches. We count it a high honor and privilege from the Lord to be able to glean from such an adventurer as Pastor Tommy Barnett.

And now you can, too! Through this book you will journey together with him among the truths, principles and experiences that have spanned almost five decades of world-changing ministry with integrity.

Pastor Barnett recently celebrated his twentieth anniversary of pastoring Phoenix First Assembly. We, his pastoral staff, thought it would be fitting preparation of your heart for the adventure of this book to read what many great leaders have said about this master adventurer.

> While others would camp on a twenty-year milestone—not you. You keep climbing...
>
> —RICK GODWIN

> The kingdom work you are doing is propelling the people of God into new realms and levels.
>
> —T. D. JAKES

> Not only have you been dynamic, but you have sustained your efforts for the kingdom at an unwavering pace that has left those of us looking on breathless.
>
> —BILL MCCARTNEY

In all my years I have seldom seen a man so dedicated and impressionable in the work of God.

—LOU RAWLS

We all need and desire leaders to challenge and inspire us. Tommy has been that ...

—CASEY TREAT

I want to go on record and say in absolute terms that you are a continual source of inspiration to me. I've never known anyone with greater zeal for the Lord.

—JAMES ROBISON

While it's true that all Tommy has accomplished has been by the help and grace of God, it's also true that these things have been accomplished because he has been doggedly faithful to a divine determination.

—BILL WILSON

We congratulate you on an extraordinary ministry that has set a real precedent in the whole body of Christ.

—DR. DAVID YONGGI CHO

In my opinion, you have become one of the most respected Christian leaders in America today.

—STEPHEN STRANG

You have set a marvelous example for the next generation and have greatly impacted multitudes in the past twenty years.

—DAVID WILKERSON

Now, let the Lord inspire you as you adventure yourself in the pages of this book.

Introduction

An Appetite for Adventure

THE CLIMBING EXPEDITION had almost reached the top. Severe cold knifed through their skin and icicles formed on their eyelashes. The air was so thin that their minds had slowed to the mental pace of children. Yet the adventurous group trudged upward toward the highest point on earth. It was 1996, and the team was determined that nothing would stop them. One by one they stepped onto the summit of Mt. Everest, snapped a few photos and began the harsh descent.

In some places, ice replaced snow as they rammed their spiked climbing boots into the ground with each step. Used oxygen containers rolled down the mountain, as if scampering to safety. Their hearts beat faster as the winds picked up, and they sensed a vicious storm coming at their expedition. Within hours, eight from the party were dead, and others were badly frostbitten in a sporting accident that would again thrust Mt. Everest into the headlines as a killer.

Leading one of the three expeditions up the behemoth mass of stone and snow that day was Scott Fischer, an experienced climber legendary for his strength and drive. This time, however, the results proved fatally different. The snowstorm, sub-zero temperatures and winds in excess of seventy miles per hour were a recipe for disaster for even the expert mountaineer.

Scott and ten other people perished that day on the side of the mountain dubbed "the roof of the world." Would this latest tragedy serve as a warning to others, keeping them away from Everest? No. *The woman who purchased the mountain expedition company from Fischer's estate reports that client interest has grown "significantly."*

Why would someone be attracted to climbing a mountain when the chances are great he could lose his life? And why would he choose to go with a company whose founder *died* in a mountain climbing incident? Despite the widely publicized deaths, Mt. Everest remains the choice of those in search of an adventure.

A FIXATION FOR ADVENTURE

Would you climb Mt. Everest if given the chance? I'm sure many of you would. I believe the human body and spirit are wired for adventure. God has given us an innate desire to take risks. And yet, Americans are bored with life. Knowledge, convenience and leisure are plentiful. But the urge to live adventurously remains strong.

Some people try to experience adventure vicariously by watching television shows. One current show promises real-life "dangerous chases and crashes." Another lights up the screen with "never-before-seen footage [of] unexpected explosions destroying buildings and cars, and missiles misfiring with terrifying results." Yet another features video of "recreational activities that take a turn for the worse, including an octopus attacking a diver." And another shows "graphic, caught-on-tape accounts of pets and performing animals turning on their owners and handlers. Among the footage: a pet alligator chomping down on his owner's head, a trained elephant running amok, two horses fighting and a performing killer whale attacking its trainer."[1]

I don't watch much television, but many people tune into these shows week after week.

Some people want to experience danger themselves. I saw an article recently about individuals who pay large sums of money to participate in a summer camp where they get to behave like secret agents. They drive around the Arizona desert in all-terrain vehicles, conduct espionage missions against other teams, fire paint balls at each other and "rescue" hostages.[2] According to a 1997 report by the Travel Industry Association of America, ninety-eight million American adults took an adventure vacation in the last five years. That comprises 50 percent of the traveling population. While some people find a challenge in scaling a towering mountain, others find a thrill in observing rare mountain gorillas in their natural habitats, river rafting in the backwoods of Alaska, volcano climbing or shark diving.

Some people go even further, diving from skyscrapers and tall cliffs with only parachutes on their backs. One man, supposedly an expert in this type of sport, died recently when unexpected winds drove him into a cliff. And yet people continue to jump, even doing so in honor of their deceased colleague.

We are becoming a culture fixated on perverse forms of adventure. We're on a mission, searching for an ever-increasing adrenaline rush.

What is it that drives us to take death-defying vacations, to watch shows where people and animals are hurt and maimed, to force ourselves to stare death in the face? I believe people are looking for the ultimate challenge—an adventure that gives purpose and meaning to life in a time when luxury has not been the handmaiden of happiness we thought it would be.

We crave a challenge that is worth dying for.

THE GREATEST ADVENTURE OF ALL

Despite popular opinion, the Christian life is intended to be the greatest adventure of all. I've heard people say so many times, "I've thought about being a Christian, but the Christian life is so boring." When I hear those words, I know that such an individual has settled for a false religion, certainly not the kind of Christianity I know. G. K. Chesterton, the famous English author, once wrote: "The Christian faith has not been tried and found wanting. It has been found difficult and left untried." How true that is today.

Look at the original disciples. John was boiled in oil, then exiled on the isle of Patmos. Peter was crucified upside down, and Peter's wife was martyred as well. Andrew was crucified on an X-shaped cross. James was martyred. Philip was imprisoned and crucified. Nathanael (also known as Bartholomew) was cruelly beaten and crucified upside down. Thomas was impaled by pagans with a spear. Matthew was killed with a pickax. James the Less was beaten, stoned and had his head bashed in with a hammer. Thaddeus (also known as Jude) was crucified, as was Simon. The apostle Paul, who had written, "Follow my example as I follow the example of Christ," was martyred in Rome. Each of these men lived a life brimming with adventure before God allowed them to be martyred.

This doesn't sound like a Saturday quilting club religion to me! And yet what has happened to us that we live so differently from the apostles? We have settled for the world's adventures and left God's adventures for the history books.

God has perfectly tailored adventures for every person on the planet. Some adventures are more dangerous than others. Some even demand your life.

A Thirst for Something More

Do you thirst for God-given adventure? Do you hunger for more than TV-show faith? Do you want to live for a cause that's worth dying for?

In this book I want to invite you to step out of weak religion into God's greatest adventure. My desire is that you will be encouraged to embark on a path unencumbered by small dreams. I want to show you the Christian life the way God intended it.

ADVENTURE YOURSELF

I want you to adventure yourself!

My hope is that you will be inspired to abandon unsatisfying adventures. As you discover your true purpose, I pray that you will be inspired to join the greatest Adventurer of all, Jesus, on a journey that will take your breath away.

ONE

Dreams Delayed Come True

Every man dies, but not every man lives.

—WILLIAM WALLACE

HAS GOD GIVEN you a dream? Has He projected a great adventure onto the screen of your heart? Has He planted the seed of a Holy Spirit-inspired plan in your soul? If so, then you and I have something in common. And yet, sometimes dreams seem like illusions, don't they? We wonder if they will ever come true. Like you, I know what it's like to walk in the fields of my heart and say, "But God, nothing is growing!" and to hear Him say, "Just wait. The seeds of adventure are just below the surface."

For over forty years, the seeds of two adventures remained buried deep in my heart. I longed to fulfill these dreams, but the time delayed in coming. As you can imagine, I was often miserable, but I looked in the Bible and found I was not alone in playing the waiting game. The prophet Habakkuk spoke of such times:

> For the vision is yet for an appointed time;
> But at the end it will speak, and it will not lie.
> Though it tarries, wait for it;
> Because it will surely come,
> It will not tarry.
>
> —HABAKKUK 2:3

In my situation, both adventures burst into my life without warning and came to pass through God's creative plan. One of those dreams was fulfilled, and the other is continuing to be fulfilled. I know that you too have a dreamer's heart, and that is why I am eager to share my experiences with you.

THE TWO DREAMS IN MY HEART

Dream #1: Build an international church.

Big cities have always caught my fancy. I tend to live by the maxim of "the bigger the better," and big cities give me a visual picture of what big dreamers—architects and designers—can do. When I was a teenager, I spent the winters in school like the other kids, but when summer rolled around, I didn't join the Little League team—I traveled the country preaching revivals. At the close of a particular revival I was holding in New York City at age eighteen, I decided to stay a few extra days to see the sights of that wonderful city.

Anyone who owns a television knows what New York City looks like, but to me, being there was a lesson in adventurous living, from the traffic to the subways to the street vendors speaking every imaginable language. I visited the grand lady of American freedom, the Statue of Liberty, standing proudly in the Hudson Bay. I took the elevator to the top of the Empire State Building and surveyed the incomparable Manhattan skyline. I caught a baseball game at Yankee Stadium. The sights, smells and energy of the city were unforgettable.

But what impressed me most, among all of New York's jewels, was the United Nations building. Situated along the East River in Manhattan and completed just a few years earlier, the heavily glassed building took my breath away with its architectural grandeur and air of international importance. Inside was an open area where dignitaries sat during the various United Nations sessions. In the back, separated by glass partitions, people of different ethnic groups could sit and listen to the proceedings in their native tongues. French, German, Spanish, Korean—every language could be interpreted for the listener.

Awed by what I saw, I thought to myself, *Someday I'm going to build a church here just like this that reaches all languages and cultures. I want to pastor it and call it the New York International Church.*

No sooner had I tucked that dream away than my travels took me to Miami, and I decided I would like to build an international church there, too. Soon after that I visited Los Angeles and remarked to myself, *Someday I would like to build a Los Angeles International Church as well.* In fact, in all the great cities of America I was privileged to preach in, I wanted to build international churches to reach people of different ethnic groups. I would climb to the roof of any big-city hotel I was staying in, look over the city and pray, "God, send someone to this city." In every city, I felt God wanted to build a *Dream Center.*

When I sensed God leading me to the pastorate, I thought my time for big-city ministry had come, and I sent my name to all the churches in major cities, but none of them had a position for me. My bags were packed for *Bigtown, USA,* but my train was heading for the sticks. God was not allowing me to go to New York or Miami or Los Angeles. Eventually I accepted a pastorate in Davenport, Iowa, a city with a population of ninety thousand. I was puzzled and maybe a little disappointed. I loved the people there, but why was I pastoring in Davenport if God had put dreams the size of New York in my heart?

About eight years later, after a significant and sustained revival in Davenport, God led me to a church in Phoenix. Finally, when I was fifty-seven years old, he added a church in Los Angeles to my already full schedule at Phoenix First Assembly. The birth of the Los Angeles International Church—known as the Dream Center—was the fulfillment of a forty-year-old dream. I want to discuss that dream more later, but let me mention my second dream here. Actually, the first dream of having an international church became the very reason my second great dream was fulfilled.

Dream #2: Run across the country.

When I was in high school, I competed on the track team as a long distance runner. Because by nature I wasn't very fast, I competed in the mile run, the two-mile run and cross country, which demanded endurance more than speed.

One day I thought, *I would like to run across America—from New York City to Los Angeles—and hold revivals in the major cities along the way.* This was long before jogging became popular and before people were reading Dennis Jenkins' *Walk Across America.*

As an evangelist, I was intent on reaching America with the gospel and winning souls to Christ. I knew the publicity generated from a run like that would certainly attract people to my nightly meetings. But because I was always so busy preaching and the time commitment was so great, I was never able to fit the running adventure into my busy schedule. The seed of that adventure lay in the ground of my heart, waiting on God.

On my sixtieth birthday, however, I fulfilled this dream after a delay of forty-four years! In order to raise money to renovate the building we had purchased for the Dream Center, I decided to jog and walk from Phoenix to Los Angeles and receive pledges for my journey. No, I didn't start in New York as I had originally envisioned, but starting in Phoenix was good enough for me.

Two Dreams Meet in One Adventure

My run was preceded by a financial crisis. The Los Angeles International Church moved into the old Queen of Angels hospital in July 1995. We had purchased the hospital and were occupying it. But we knew we were on borrowed time because the city authorities had given us until February 1998 to bring the seventy-one-year-old building up to city code. If we couldn't, we would have to shut down the church.

It was a massive undertaking. Seven hundred rooms

needed to be refurbished and equipped with sprinklers and fire alarms. The cracked and peeling facade needed to be redone. Inside, the asbestos had to be removed from the walls and ceiling. The amount needed for repairs: a staggering $2.5 million.

On a Sunday morning, I announced to my church in Phoenix that I was going to take my two-week vacation to run the 426 miles from Phoenix to the Dream Center. Calculating that it would take 700,000 steps, I asked supporters to donate $3 a step for specific portions of the trip.

To train for my new adventure, I jogged and walked every day, sometimes as far as fifteen miles. While in L.A., my training runs took me through Koreatown, Chinatown, Japanese neighborhoods, Russian communities and Hispanic barrios. Being among the different ethnic peoples who inhabited our city touched my heart. I ran through skid row areas, passing people who lived in cardboard boxes. At times I would train at midnight, running through crime-infested neighborhoods. On street corners I observed hurting men and women peddling drugs and illicit sex. God gave me a new compassion for the people we were trying to reach at the Dream Center. As I trained, people began calling me the Forrest Gump of the gospel!

I consulted physicians to ensure my body could endure the beating of such a long run. After administering a battery of tests, my doctors gave me a clean bill of health. The Phoenix Sun's basketball team heard about my run, and their doctors and trainers became consultants for my medical team as well, proving again that when you let the world know about your adventures, they will want to join you.

The First Day of My Great Adventure

Sunday night, October 26, 1997, we kicked off my run to L.A. with a rally at Phoenix First Assembly. Thousands of people were present for my send-off, and as the service concluded, I ran down the center aisle of the auditorium to the theme song from *Rocky* and onto the busy streets of Phoenix. Behind a police escort, hundreds of people joined me on the first leg of the run. As we headed on our seven-mile run into the night, I was already on my way toward my goal of $2 million.

Invigorated by all the excitement surrounding my run, I could hardly sleep that first night. I jumped out of bed at five o'clock Monday morning and hit the ground running–literally–as I departed the retirement village of Sun City. I certainly didn't feel retired!

My first day on the road was something of a mountaintop experience, right there in the desert. My mind was clear. No one was around to disturb me as the asphalt trail stretched before me. I had no phone calls or appointments to keep. Just God, me and a gorgeous view of desert life with its birds, animals, cactuses and sturdy bushes. The rhythm of my breath and the thump of my feet against the road soothed me, and I thought, *I feel like a new man.* Ascending the mountain passes that hug Phoenix and descending into the desert again, I discovered a beauty in God's creation I had overlooked many times. In my exuberance, I ran thirty-five miles my first full day. Not bad for a man sixty years young!

But blissful Monday faded into bearish Tuesday. Before I even opened my eyes, I could feel a hundred points of pain in my feet–blisters had covered them. My muscles ached and my lower back throbbed. My rapid pace had caught up with me. Determined to go forty miles that day, I was on track at noon, having already covered twenty-one. But I would only complete another nine miles before being forced to stop.

FIRST FRUITS OF MY ADVENTURE

During my walk that difficult day, God used a divine appointment to turn my pain into praises.

Because state and federal laws forbade me from running on certain highways, I was forced to go down a desolate dirt road. Not one car passed by as I limped along my way. The sandy road acted like ball bearings beneath my hurting feet. It was only my second full day, and I was already unsure that I would be able to complete my journey. I was hurting so badly, and I felt so very alone—such a contrast to the day before when the very wind seemed to whisper my name and carry me along.

As the day dragged on, my assistant, Gary Blair, who had been following behind me in my Jeep, headed into a nearby town to pick up some supplies. I tried to keep my spirits up, so I focused on the ultimate goal of raising money for the Dream Center. Faces of needy people flashed through my mind. *Yes,* I thought, *that's where the real joy is.*

Suddenly from behind me the roar of a pickup engine tore a hole through my thoughts. I looked back over my shoulder but didn't recognize the truck. When it was near enough to pass it skidded to a halt and then followed slowly on my heels. My weary mind began conjuring up various threatening scenarios. *Here I am, all by myself, with nobody else around. What does this person want? Is he going to rob me or hurt me?*

Just then the truck pulled up beside me, and a handsome, young Native American man about thirty years old poked his head out the window and asked, "Are you OK?"

"I'm fine," I answered as I nodded my head and kept on walking

"Where are you going?"

"Los Angeles."

"You've got to be kidding!" At this point I was still 350 miles from my destination. "Why are you walking to L.A.?"

I stopped and focused my eyes on the man so I could give him a decent explanation. I was a pastor, I said, raising money to refurbish the Dream Center, a hospital for hurting people in inner-city Los Angeles.

He paused for a moment, and then with a serious look he said, "Tell me about the Dream Center."

Gladly, I thought.

"It's a place where gang members, prostitutes, drug addicts, alcoholics, runaways and homeless people can live while they get help for their problems. We accept everyone."

His eyes welled up with tears. "I think I need to go there," he said to my astonishment. "I drink too much, and I have a drug problem. Right now I'm facing a jail sentence. I've lost my family, and I don't want my little boy to grow up like this."

As I shared the gospel with this man, Gary drove up in the Jeep. "Do you know of any shortcuts that would save us some time?" Gary asked our new friend.

"Yeah, you can go through the reservation. I'll take you through it."

The man offered to get into Gary's car and guide us on

our way. "Why don't you two drive together," I suggested. "Gary, you can get directions from him. And he's got a problem maybe you two can talk about." I winked at Gary. He knew what I meant.

I continued on my journey as the two men followed behind in the Jeep. After a while I noticed that Gary had stopped the Jeep, but I kept walking. Soon they caught up with me again. Gary honked, and I looked back. "Pastor, this young man just gave his life to Christ!" A thrill ran through my aching muscles. For those brief moments, the pain in my body didn't matter anymore.

The young man called his girlfriend on our cell phone and told her what happened. She was flabbergasted, and he put me on the phone to assure her it was true.

When he got off the phone he said to me, "I want to get baptized."

"If you come to church, I'll baptize you when I get back."

"No, I want to be baptized now."

"We're in the desert. We can't baptize you."

"But I don't want to wait any longer." His insistence was sincere, and it tugged at my heart. The whole situation reminded me of the story of the Ethiopian eunuch in Acts 8.

"There's no water out here. How can I baptize you?" I said. I was willing, but we needed a creative idea.

Gary suddenly interjected, "Wait a minute." We stopped, and he got out of the Jeep. Gary opened up the trunk, pulled out a bottle of Evian water and told our new friend, "Bend over and stick out your head." Gary baptized him right there on that dusty road in the middle of the desert. Although our church doesn't baptize by sprinkling, that day we became Methodists!

Several months later the young man came to Phoenix, testified in church on a Sunday morning and was baptized in a baptismal tank. Later Gary accompanied him to court, and his jail sentence was reduced.

God had arranged for that divine appointment—an adventure I neither envisioned nor planned. However, my body still screamed with pain. By the end of that day, the blisters on my feet burst, forcing me to stop well short of my daily goal.

THE SPIRIT WAS WILLING, BUT THE FLESH WAS IN PAIN!

When I woke up Wednesday morning, I could hardly move. My feet were a mess, my hip joints were complaining horribly, and my lower back was beating a bass drum. Walking outside in the cold desert air didn't help my situation. The intensity of the pain was so severe, I thought I was going to die. As I walked, I prayed for God to give me the strength to continue.

On Tuesday I had walked mostly uphill. Now, on Wednesday, my path took me downhill, giving my feet the opportunity to blister evenly. By Wednesday night, I had covered one hundred miles—and I felt like it, too!

Time seemingly stood still as I limped toward the California border over the next couple of days. Every day at the end of my walk, I would have to be carried to the restaurant and then to my motel room. Even before I was undressed I would fall asleep. Then the next morning before the sun was up, I was back on the road again. During my rest periods, I would lie on my back, extend my legs, put ice packs on them, wrap them and have my assistants massage them. I wasn't a pretty sight, but I was determined.

On Saturday, I arrived in Parker, Arizona, on the beautiful Colorado River. My feet were raw, and I was losing my toenails. Every five miles I was forced to change socks in order to minimize blistering. I simply could go no farther.

A FOOT DOCTOR FROM HEAVEN

We decided to drive up to Lake Havasu so I could visit a foot specialist. After walking into this doctor's office I learned that he was a marathon runner. Immediately I knew God had brought us to the right place. He listened to my travails and looked at my feet. Then the doctor asked, "What size shoes do you wear?"

"Size 9."

"Well, that's part of your problem. You need size 11 shoes." He explained that feet grow throughout a person's life. My feet were really a size 10, he told me. Because they were swollen from my trek, they were now a size 11.

The doctor cut all the dead skin off my feet to give me additional room. Then he applied a protective coating of Nu-Skin to prevent further blistering. After meeting with this doctor, I bought a pair of new shoes. I felt as if I had been given a new lease on life!

A REST WITH DIVIDENDS

A few days before I left Phoenix I had received a call from the office of heavyweight boxing champion Evander Holyfield.

"Tommy," his representative began, "two days before his

next fight, Evander wants to invite the public to a rally, and he'd like you to address the crowd before he gives his testimony. He also plans on collecting food and clothing for the homeless at this rally. Then you can stick around and support him as he defends his title. Evander would like to know if you can join him."

"I'm sorry," I replied. "I can't make it because I'll be on my walk to L.A."

"If you come, we'll pay all of your expenses and put you up in a nice hotel."

"I'd love to—I really would—but I need to stick with my walk and not break it up."

"If we let you hand out pledge forms for your walk, would you come?"

"I can't."

"We'll give front row seats to the fight to you, Marja and Matthew." I must confess, I had to admire a person with such a relentless pursuit.

"I'm sorry."

"If you join him in Las Vegas, Evander will come to the Dream Center, bring food and clothes and give his testimony for a big outreach."

Now, I *can* be bought. Knowing the popularity of Evander Holyfield in the inner city, I realized the potential an event like that would have to harvest souls. So I agreed.

It turned out that this side trip to Las Vegas couldn't have come at a better time. My wife, Marja, and I spent two days there and had a wonderful time. The rally with Evander was attended by twelve thousand people, and about a thousand responded to the altar call. It was a glorious time.

The next evening Marja, Matthew and I watched the boxing match. As Evander entered the arena, much to my surprise, Christian music blared over the loudspeakers. Matthew, standing next to me, raised his hands and praised the Lord. I nudged him and said, "Son, straighten up. This isn't a revival meeting; this is a fight!" Shortly thereafter, a television commentator exclaimed, "Ladies and gentlemen, this is more like a revival than a fight!"

That night, Evander Holyfield defeated Michael Moorer and added the International Boxing Federation belt to his growing collection of world heavyweight titles. This two-day diversion provided my feet and body the rest they so desperately needed to complete my adventure. Once again, my journey became a joy.

PRESSING ON TOWARD THE GOAL

The next morning my trek across the wilderness continued. Making my way across the California back roads, God shared with me the wonders of His beauty. I viewed a dry salt lake from the distance and passed the Joshua Tree National Monument where the low Colorado Desert and the high Mojave Desert converge. These incomparable sights are etched forever into my memory.

My travels took me through desert towns like Twentynine Palms, Yucca Valley and Palm Springs. Along the way, I spoke in four churches, sharing the vision of the Dream Center. My adventure was going just as I had dreamed it would years earlier.

Soon I entered the Los Angeles metropolitan area. Running from San Bernardino to Hollywood took four days, and it was my favorite part of the run. Because I was expending so many calories, I could eat virtually anything. So I stopped at every ice cream shop I passed and enjoyed a double dip Rocky Road. I lost ten pounds during my run, but it would have been fifteen if I hadn't eaten so much ice cream at the end!

On I ran through the busy streets of cities like Fontana, Covina and Pomona. I must admit, maneuvering gets a little tricky when you have to compete with stoplights and heavy traffic. I continued through East L.A., then on to Hollywood.

THE THRILL OF THE FINISH

Finally, on Thursday, November 2—twenty-six days after I had begun—I arrived at the famous Mann's Chinese Theater in Hollywood. Hundreds of people showed up from all over the nation to welcome me. Fellow pastors, friends, people from the Dream Center and celebrities (including actress Dyan Cannon and singer Lou Rawls) were there to celebrate the end of my journey. Marja, of course, was by my side as I ran down the walk of fame.

Newspapers, television news crews and radio stations were on hand to cover the story. After a news conference, I was joined by many of my wonderful supporters for the final seven miles of my run. We jogged down Hollywood Boulevard and onto Sunset Boulevard, which lies just two blocks from the Dream Center.

We entered the Dream Center grounds to a cheering throng of supporters throwing confetti and waving welcome signs. Running beneath a big arch of balloons, I felt like a marathon runner who had just won the Olympics. It was one of the most glorious days of my life. The lost toenails, blistered feet, aching muscles, sunburn and weight loss were worth it all.

At the Dream Center that night we held what I called "the mother of all celebrations." In the end, my run raised $750,000 dollars for the Dream Center. Not bad for three weeks of work!

THE SEEDS OF ADVENTURES

Adventures begin as seeds. Like the seeds in the parable of the sower in Matthew 13, some adventures are sown into the soil of hard, skeptical hearts and never have an opportunity to flourish. *God could never use me to accomplish an adventure* **that** *big. I'm not talented enough to pull it off. What if I fail? What if God doesn't bail me out?* Immediately quashed, these seeds of adventure survive only as dim memories.

Other seeds of adventures fall on rocky soil. The budding adventurer receives the dream with joy and plans for its fulfillment. But as obstacles arise and faith is tested, the dreamer questions the validity of the adventure. *Is the adventure worth the effort? I'm not sure I'm willing to make a sacrifice like that.* Caught in the balance between counting the cost and abandoning the dream, the would-be adventurer chooses to abort. Too much work, too many hassles, too little time, too few resources, too long of a wait.

Some seeds of adventures are birthed in soil that is permeated with the worries and cares of this world. *What will people say when they hear about my dream? What if they criticize it? Will they think I'm out of my mind? What if my family and my friends object?* Trying to satisfy public opinion, the adventure becomes so diluted that it barely resembles the original idea.

But some seeds of adventures fall on good soil. There

they remain buried for a time. The adventurer waits patiently for life to burst forth. *Because I believe this dream is an adventure from God, I'm going to give Him a chance to bring it to fruition. I won't give up on the dream! Though the dream tarries, I'll wait for it because it will surely come.* Waiting patiently and prayerfully, the dream takes root and eventually yields fruit many times greater than that which was sown.

I believe that if a person can hold on to a dream five years, it will come true. *An adventure delayed is not an adventure denied.* We must learn that simply because a dream does not materialize the moment it is conceived does not mean it won't happen. Some dreams just take more time than others. On the other hand, if we do not hold onto our dreams for the long haul, we can virtually guarantee their demise.

DELAYED DREAMS DON'T DIE

My adventure through the desert was a dream delayed for forty-four years. The establishment of the Los Angeles International Church was a dream delayed for forty years. Though the fulfillment of those dreams tarried for half my life, I held onto them, and they eventually came to pass. I know that you have dreams in your heart also, and if you are like me, there are days when you wonder if they will really come forth as God said they would. I am here to tell you that in God's time, they will. He does not bury seeds to forget about them.

A famous adventurer, President Theodore Roosevelt, gives us some good advice about getting on with our adventures:

It is not the critic who counts, not the person who points out where the doer of deeds could have done better. The credit belongs to the person who is actually in the arena; whose face is marred by dust and sweat and blood; who strives valiantly; who errs and comes up short again and again; who knows the great enthusiasms, the devotions, and spends himself or herself in a worthy cause; who at best knows in the end the triumph of high achievement; and at the worst, at least fails while daring greatly; so that his or her place shall never be with those cold and timid souls who know neither victory or defeat.[1]

The prize goes to the person who understands that an adventure delayed is not an adventure denied. Go with me further down this path of adventure as we discover God's plan for every believer.

TWO

The Great Adventure

A ship in harbor is safe, but that is not what ships are built for.

—JOHN SHEDD

I WOKE UP IN a cold sweat. Thrills of fear ran up and down my body as I stared at our bedroom ceiling.

I'm going to tell them no, I thought. *I can't do this. Moving to L.A. would be too great a risk.*

I stumbled to the bathroom, closed the door and turned the light on. *I'm not a young man any more,* I thought. *It's late in my career. I don't have room to fail. What if I blow it? I'll look like a fool.*

I stared in the mirror at a fifty-seven-year-old man who had spent his life taking on one adventure after another. But this one seemed too big.

Why put your reputation in jeopardy? I asked myself, keeping quiet so as not to wake up my wife, Marja. *Why not stay put? No one would blame you. You've got a church to run, a full schedule of speaking engagements, a pastors' school and over two hundred ministries operating out of Phoenix First. They can't possibly expect you to do anything more.*

My own fear surprised me. During the day I was much more adventurous. I could see the possibilities, believe the dreams and convince myself to go for it. But when dusk turned to night, my doubts sometimes got the upper hand. I felt my night shirt clinging to my damp skin.

Tell them you prayed about it and feel that it's not God's will...

But that would be a lie.

Tell them you just bought property to build your dream house in Flagstaff.

I can't say that to godly men like these. Besides, they know me too well. They know I'm a risk-taker, and they'll keep after me until I agree.

Tell them to give you a few more days to decide...

Tell them someone else could do the same job...

Tell them anything!

I crawled back in bed, hoping my mind would spin itself out. The adventure was beginning to haunt my sleep.

THE CALL TO ADVENTURE

The decision to get involved with the church in Los Angeles was one of the most difficult I ever made. This spiritually taxing time began on a sunny Phoenix day in late 1991. The superintendent of the Southern California District of the Assemblies of God sounded somewhat mysterious on the phone.

"Tommy," Ray Rachels began, "George Wood and I would like to fly out and talk with you. Would there be a time when you could fit us into your schedule?" Of course I would meet with them. My curiosity was certainly piqued because Ray was evasive about the intent of our meeting, and I detected a slight urgency in his voice.

Following our short conversation, my mind raced. *What would our upcoming conversation be about? Why would the Southern California District Superintendent want to talk to me? And George Wood, who at the time was the Assistant Superintendent of Southern California—why was he coming to see me?* The more I thought about it, the more I wondered if I had done something wrong. For years my methods of building churches were unconventional and had raised a few eyebrows. Whatever it was, I knew it must be important, because neither of them had ever come to visit me here at church.

I was grateful when the meeting day finally arrived. Ray and George cut to the chase. "We're embarrassed even to ask this of you after seeing the beautiful campus you have here. But we believe God has called you to come to Los Angeles."

I was shocked, but I kept on listening. "L.A. is a vital city. In the last decade it has grown from seven million to almost ten million. Reports predict L.A. will house more than ten million people shortly before the turn of the century. Los Angeles is truly the melting pot of the world. Living within its limits are the largest Mexican population outside of Mexico, the largest Korean population outside of Korea and ethnic groups from twenty more countries who can say the same thing. Nearly a million and a half African Americans are in L.A. as well."

It was obvious Ray and George had done their homework. "It is the communication and entertainment hub of the world. And although it houses some of America's great universities, it is also the drug and gang capital of the world, as well as a prominent center for pornography. Los Angeles is a city where murder, abortion, crime and cults abound.

"Fifteen Assembly churches minister in the downtown area. Right now only one exceeds membership of one hundred in the Los Angeles section of the Southern California district. We need a great church in the inner city.

"Tommy, you pastor one of the largest churches in the world, and we feel that in order to penetrate this bastion of need, we need a man with your heart for the hurting. We're asking you to resign from your church in Phoenix and come to L.A. to start a new work. And to get you started, we'll give you the Bethel Temple church building in Echo Park."

To be honest, my initial inward response was, *Get thee behind me, Satan!* Of course, I couldn't say that to Ray and George! Undeterred by my nonverbal messages, they asked me, "Would you pray about it?"

"Yes, I'll pray about," I responded, "but it won't do any good."

ANSWERING THE CALL TO ADVENTURE

The first wrestling match was with my own desires. Why would I want to leave the church I loved? God had blessed us with continued growth since I had arrived in 1979. Our annual Pastors' School was the largest in the world, and we had started a Pastors College. The Master's Commission concept developed at our church was making a difference in countless churches around the world. One of our ministries, Athletes in Mission (AIM), was reaching athletes on both the professional and amateur levels. The National Association of Marriage Enhancement (NAME), which began at our church, was bringing husbands and wives together in greater intimacy. And two hundred other ministries were making a remarkable difference in Phoenix.

But in keeping with my word to Ray and George, I prayed. And after bringing this need before God, I felt impressed to go look at the area they had spoken about. So Marja and I spent part of our Christmas vacation in 1991 driving through the Los Angeles area. We made four additional trips there, and every time we surveyed the area, we were struck by the raw discouragement of the people.

I recalled that when I was nineteen, I had held a revival at the same Bethel Temple church that George and Ray offered to me. At that time it was one of the largest churches in California. During that revival in 1958 God had whispered in my heart, "You're going to pastor here someday." But by 1991 the church building had fallen into disrepair, partly due to the white flight to the suburbs. Rev. Howard Barfoot, the pastor, had faithfully served the church family there for twenty years and was ready to retire, leaving behind a small Asian church with limited funds. That would be my church.

Still, I couldn't get this city out of my heart. The more I prayed about it, the more a vision for Los Angeles became a part of me.

Once I was convinced I should be involved in the L.A. church, a year and a half later, I called Ray and George. "I think it's God's will that I should go," I began. "But rather than give up my beloved church family in Phoenix, I'll just double my load. I'll spend two days a week in Los Angeles, and I'll work five days in Phoenix. Then I'll find another pastor to work with me in order to get this church in L.A. off the ground."

They agreed to my plan, and the adventure began.

A GOD-SIZED CHALLENGE

After accepting the offer, I took inventory of my newest challenge: the daunting job of reaching inner-city Los Angeles from scratch. At age fifty-seven, I faced one of my life's greatest challenges.

Where would I begin? How would the finances come together for the kind of ministry I felt God was calling me to pursue? Where would I find the people to undertake this venture? Who would pastor the work with me?

For me, true adventure begins when the challenge I face is greater than I could ever accomplish on my own. A true adventure must be strengthened by the power of God in order to succeed. I choose not to live within the safe confines of my own abilities because then I limit God's opportunity to move. Was I ready for an adventure of this magnitude? Although I had my concerns, I knew this challenge was just another part of the adventure of serving Jesus.

And I am convinced that what has been true for me is also true for every person.

You see, I believe life is an adventure. When my alarm

goes off in the morning, I can't wait to get out of bed, because I don't know what adventurous possibilities await me. Because I try to live beyond my comfort zone, I never know how God is going to respond to my need. That's what makes the Christian life exciting!

START YOUR ADVENTURE

King David lived the life of a true adventurer. No other king in Israel's history experienced the success he did or relied more on God. A glimpse of his close life with God is revealed in a psalm that he wrote:

> Trust in the Lord, and do good;
> Dwell in the land, and feed on His faithfulness.
> Delight yourself also in the LORD,
> And He shall give you the desires of your heart.
> Commit your way to the LORD,
> Trust also in Him,
> And He shall bring it to pass.
>
> —PSALM 37:3–5

Three important principles strike me about this passage.

Principle #1: God will never lead you where you do not desire to go.

God "shall give you the desires of your heart." He's not in the business of making you go where you don't want to go. He's not going to make you become a missionary to Africa against your will. He won't call you into a vocation that you don't enjoy. But that doesn't mean He just goes along with your ideas either. If He does want to lead you where you don't want to go, He'll begin by changing your heart.

While I was thinking and praying about going to Los Angeles, I agonized over the decision of whether or not to add another project to my already busy schedule. One minute I would think, *Yes, I'm supposed to go to Los Angeles.* The next minute I would think, *No, I don't want to go to Los Angeles. It's just too great a risk.* There were many sleepless nights, but looking back, I see how God had planted the seeds for the vision behind the Dream Center and the Los Angeles International Church in my heart years before when I was only nineteen. Then, as I sought God, He brought about a change in my heart so that my desires became His.

Principle #2: God gives you an adventure all your own.

Just as no two people in the world are exactly alike, no two adventures from God are alike either. He has tailored a unique adventure just for you. That's what makes being a Christian so exciting. The psalmist wrote:

> For you created my inmost being;
>> you knit me together in my mother's womb.
> I praise you because I am fearfully and wonderfully
>> made;
>> your works are wonderful,
>> I know that full well.
> My frame was not hidden from you
>> when I was made in the secret place.
> When I was woven together in the depths of the
>> earth,
>> your eyes saw my unformed body.

> All the days ordained for me
> were written in your book
> before one of them came to be.
> —PSALM 139:13–16, NIV

The innermost part of your personality—your inmost being—was a special creation, a limited edition from God. In your mother's womb, God knit you into the person He wanted you to be. Furthermore, all your days were ordained by God. Your heavenly Father has been intimately involved in your development and destiny ever since you were a gleam in your earthly father's eye!

God created you with a unique blend of passions, personality traits and gifts for a special purpose. And because there is no one quite like you, God has a unique adventure perfectly designed for your strengths.

Missionaries tell me, "Tommy, I feel sorry that you have to stay here in the United States and pastor people who have heard the gospel before. I get to blaze new trails for the gospel in places never before reached."

I tell them, "I feel sorry for you because you miss out on all the excitement of pastoring a congregation and making a difference in the lives of self-centered Americans!"

You see, God gives every person the opportunity to live his or her personal dream. I am pursuing my passion: sharing the gospel with the destitute in the city. And I get to utilize my personality and gifts in order to do that. As pastor of Phoenix First Assembly and associate pastor of the Los Angeles International Church, my job is to help people pursue the dreams God has already planted in their hearts.

The two principles above—that God will never lead you

where you don't want to go and that God has tailored a unique adventure all your own—rest firmly on a third important principle:

Principle #3: The key to embarking on your unique adventure is submission to God.

Look at the commands David gives us in Psalm 37: trust, dwell, feed, delight, commit and trust again. Trust is mentioned twice—at the beginning and at the end of the list. That means the adventure is going to require a measure of faith.

D. L. Moody once said, "It is yet to be seen what God can do with a man who will yield himself completely to God." Truthfully, even I have many secret areas that have not been given up to God. Yet I long to be the person who gives more of his life to God than anyone else does.

Trust means relying on God—it also means giving control of our lives to him. We're not the masters of own destinies. God is. As we dwell in His presence, feed on His Word, enjoy Him and commit our ways to Him, He will conform our desires to His. That's when the adventure begins!

Take a moment to ask yourself:

· Is fear keeping me from my God-given adventure?
· Are the doubts that swarm me in the night defeating my dreams?
· Is my ship of destiny in the harbor, not making its way toward the open sea?

Now is a good time to trust God for the miraculous. Now is the time to adventure yourself.

THREE

Make a Difference in Your World

To every man there comes in his lifetime that special moment when he is figuratively tapped on the shoulder and offered that chance to do a very special thing, unique to him and fitted to his talents.

—WINSTON CHURCHILL

ONE MORNING IN the little college town of Waxahachie, Texas, a scrawny, 130-pound young man sat in the chapel service at Southwestern Bible College (now Southwestern University) listening to a man preach. I don't remember the preacher's name, and I don't even remember the premise of his sermon. But I do remember that his text was Jude 20–22:

> But ye, beloved, building up yourselves on your most holy faith, praying in the Holy Ghost, keep yourselves in the love of God, looking for the mercy of our Lord Jesus Christ unto eternal life. And of some

have compassion, *making a difference…*

—KJV, EMPHASIS ADDED

In *Your* World

In his sermon he made a statement that penetrated the deepest part of my heart. "You can make a difference…" Do you know what my first reaction was? *I could never do that.* I was so much smaller than everyone else my age back then. I was shy, introverted and somewhat insecure. Yet this man had the audacity to act as if even I could make a difference in my world. I thought that might have been true for others, but not for me.

Then immediately he added, "…in *your* world."

Instantly I responded to myself, *I can do that.*

At that time my world was very small. On weekends I'd preach in little outreach churches to twenty or thirty people at the most. Once I preached before a congregation of one hundred, and it seemed like an enormous church to me. You see, my world at that time was a little smaller than it is now.

When the preacher in that chapel service was finished, and everyone else had gone off to class, I knelt at the altar in the corner and prayed, "Dear God, I promise You that I'm going to make a difference in my world."

I didn't believe I could make a difference in *the* world, but I did believe I could make a difference in *my* world. You see, until you make a difference in *your* world, you'll never be able to make a difference in *the* world.

When Jesus ascended into heaven, He promised His followers:

> But you will receive power when the Holy Spirit comes on you; and you will be my witnesses in Jerusalem, and in all Judea and Samaria, and to the ends of the earth.
>
> —ACTS 1:8, NIV

Before the early church could turn the world upside down, they first had to make a difference in their own backyard—Jerusalem. And from Jerusalem, the young believers moved into Judea, then into Samaria, and then to the ends of the earth. That's the story of the spread of the gospel from the time of Christ until today.

You may have big dreams of reaching the world for Jesus Christ. You may see yourself speaking before thousands of spellbound people and conducting large conferences for church leaders. You may want to preach the gospel, build a great church, take the Good News to a foreign field and make a difference in the world. But I ask you, "Are you making a difference in your *present* world?"

On the other hand, you may be like I was. You may wish you could make a difference in your world, but you're plagued with feelings of doubt and low self-esteem. *How could I ever make a difference? How could God ever use me?* My encouragement to you is this: Don't concern yourself about making a difference in the world right now—just start making a difference in *your* world.

STARTING OUT SMALL

The first part of my ministry was spent as an itinerant evangelist. I traveled preaching the gospel throughout America and around the world, and by the grace of God, I

31

experienced a great harvest of souls. When I sensed God calling me to be a pastor, as I already mentioned, I contacted all the Assemblies of God churches located in major cities who were seeking a pastor. Only one church responded, and here is what they told me: "Evangelists don't make good pastors."

Undeterred, I contacted churches in medium-sized cities, but again, I received no response. Despite my passion for the big city, I settled for contacting churches in any community, regardless of numbers or population. Do you see how my dream was getting downsized? Only one church responded—a small congregation of seventy-six in Davenport, Iowa. Because I had decided I would go to whichever church would have me, I accepted their offer and treated my assignment as if it were in a major city. I figured God could do whatever He wanted, wherever He wanted.

God blessed our work there, and we mushroomed into one of the fastest growing churches in America. We were influential in shutting down the massage parlors and dirty bookstores. One Sunday, we rented the John O'Donnell baseball stadium and broke the record for the world's largest Sunday school with twenty-five thousand people present. Johnny Cash sang, I preached and five thousand people responded to the salvation message. It was the largest crowd ever assembled in Davenport up to that time. We started out small, but by the time I left, we had grown to a congregation of four thousand people. Church leaders began coming to me and asking, "What's the secret to your success?" So I started an annual three-day Tommy Barnett's Pastors' School so other churches could catch our vision for making a difference.

ENLARGING MY WORLD

Then God called me to Phoenix, Arizona, and my world got bigger. Now I was in a metropolitan area of over two million people. I moved from a blue-collar city to a white-collar city. Immediately our church of two hundred began to grow as we sought to make a difference in our own world. You see, what God has blessed in our church is simply the fact that our people seek to make a difference in *their* world.

We continued the Pastors' School in Phoenix, and last year over seven thousand men and women attended, despite the fact that we spent little on advertising. We also started the Master's Commission—a one-year, full-time discipleship school designed to instill within young people a desire to follow Jesus Christ and make a difference in *their* world. Mornings are spent in scripture memorization and Bible study, and the rest of the day is spent ministering to hurting people. Today, eighty-five affiliate Master's Commission schools network together around the world to reach hundreds of thousands of people a year for Christ. Two years ago we started the Phoenix Pastors College, a two-year accredited college to train ministers.

Currently, Phoenix First Assembly reaches tens of thousands of hurting people every week through over two hundred ministries, ranging from our bus ministry under the direction of Jeff Allaway to Athletes International, our ministry to world-class athletes, under the direction of Larry Kerychuk.

Attendance at Phoenix First Assembly is now more than fifteen thousand and growing. Recently, *Time* magazine named us one of the top ten largest churches in the nation.

We praise God for the success we have experienced, but we also understand that one of the key ingredients to our effectiveness is a church full of people making a difference in *their* world, which leads to them making a difference in *the* world.

Do you see how it works?

As we are faithful in making a difference in our world, God enlarges it. Don't fret about how big or small your world is—just make a difference where you are. As you do, your world and your circle of influence will grow. You don't have to have a degree from some Bible college to do that. All you need is a heart after God and a desire to make a difference.

When God called me to Los Angeles, my world got even bigger. I didn't want to bite off more than I could chew. But enlarging your world includes being stretched. I have never been busier, nor have I ever been as tired when I go to bed as I am now. But neither have I ever felt such a great sense of adventure.

SEEING THE WORLD FROM GOD'S PERSPECTIVE

Before deciding whether or not to expand into Los Angeles, Marja and I scouted out the land. We drove the freeways of Los Angeles and explored the varied ethnic neighborhoods. A wealthy entrepreneur flew us over the city in his helicopter. From above, he pointed out, "There's Koreatown...that's where the Cambodians live," and so on.

On the ground, the city felt ominous because all we could see were houses, buildings and people. Driving the vast arteries of the city, our dream of reaching downtown Los Angeles appeared virtually unattainable. But from the air, the city took on an entirely new perspective. When we saw the city from above, somehow it grew smaller and didn't seem so intimidating. That helped me see that *our world is only as big as our perspective.*

When we survey our world from *our* perspective, obstacles often appear much bigger than they really are. But from God's perspective, they aren't nearly as big. Mountains aren't so great, valleys aren't so deep, buildings aren't so tall and distances aren't so far. From below, the concept of making a difference in Los Angeles could seem impractical and unworkable, but from above, it wasn't so far-fetched.

Because our pilot knew the Los Angeles area, I asked him, "Where do you think we should build?"

"Don't build downtown. Others have tried it and failed."

Although he was able to see Los Angeles from a high perspective, when it came to a spiritual vantage point, he could only see at ground level.

A Surprising Choice

Starting the church in L.A. was full of challenges, not the least of which was finding another pastor to work with me there. I contacted many leading pastors and invited them to join me in making a difference. Some felt called to stay with their congregations, and others were interested until they learned the church would be in the inner city. I was running into closed doors everywhere.

One day a man in my church told me I should take my son Matthew to Los Angeles to pastor with me. This idea was seconded by another. I remembered that from the time he was a child, Matthew felt the call to pastoral ministry. Because of his call, he would often forego activities with his friends while growing up so he could spend time with me learning the ins and outs of ministry. On Sunday nights when his peers went out for ice cream, Matthew would wait for me after the service so we could drive home together and discuss what happened in church that day.

Although he was young—not even twenty—I knew there was a definite call on his life. When I suggested he help pastor the L.A. International Church, his eyes lit up. I didn't know that four years earlier God had told him that by the time he was twenty, he would be pastoring in Los Angeles.

In September 1994, we had our first worship service with forty-eight precious Filipinos in the historic Bethel Temple, the first Assembly of God church in Los Angeles that was birthed out of the Azusa Street Revival of the early 1900s. That day, Matthew was the only blonde, blue-eyed boy in the audience as well as in the neighborhood.

As good as I felt about our first worship service at Bethel Temple was how guilty I felt about leaving. Driving to the airport to catch a plane back for Phoenix, I asked myself, *Am I setting Matthew up for failure?* Here was a twenty-year-old man—barely out of his teens—replacing an eighty-three-year-old pastor with over half a century of ministry experience. This quaint church jumped from having the oldest Assemblies of God pastor to the youngest.

Just like his father years before, Matthew's only experience coming into his first pastorate was that of an evangelist. And like his father, he faced similar obstacles.

Early on Matthew realized that making a difference in

his world wasn't going to be easy. Although the Bethel Temple building was located in a Hispanic neighborhood, the congregation was composed of older Filipinos who were afraid of Hispanics. Matthew sought to reach his "Jerusalem," but he encountered immediate resistance from his own people who wanted nothing to do with them. Leery of the "alien" church in their neighborhood, the Hispanics were reluctant to come.

Suspicious of their young pastor, the congregation began unraveling, and attendance plummeted to fifteen. My heart ached for my son as my greatest concern was realized. In those early days I would call him on the phone to console him or give any advice he might need. Whenever I asked how he was doing, he responded that he was "fine" or "wonderful." I knew he wanted to quit, but he chose not to dwell on the negative.

Many pastors would have packed their bags and moved on, but Matthew was determined not to allow this stalemate to stop him. From the outset, Matthew decided he wasn't going to build a church in the boardroom; he was going to build a church by meeting the needs of people in the surrounding community.

And what better way to find out the needs of your community than by placing yourself in the middle of where your world walks by? Blessed with some of the most temperate weather on earth, Matthew took a very unconventional approach and set up his office on the sidewalk in front of the church.

To every person who walked by, Matthew would look up from his work and say, *"Hola,"* which is Spanish for "hello." Because of the unusual appearance, his greeting often spurred further conversations with the very people he was trying to reach. And the questions they asked—"Who are you?" and "Why do you have a desk outside?"—opened the door for sharing his heart with the neighborhood and discovering what their needs were. Matthew issued an appeal to the church members in a sermon titled "Putting Yourself in Another Man's World." Modeling his challenge, he put himself in the middle of his community and made the people in his neighborhood his people.

He made their language his language—for an hour each day he was tutored in Spanish. He made their food his food. He made their favorite sport, soccer, his favorite sport.

In a vacant lot nearby, he poured a concrete slab, transforming it into a basketball court. Out of the woodwork the gang members started appearing. On the basketball court there is no prejudice; what matters most is skill. So Matthew, who was recruited out of high school by a number of colleges to play basketball, earned the respect of the gang members by his play on the court. Building on his success, he poured another slab of concrete and constructed a platform for weights and an outdoor gym.

Through a tragic gang shooting Matthew ministered to the deceased man's family and fellow gang members, earning their acceptance and trust. More people from the neighborhood emerged, and slowly, they started coming to the church, many of them getting saved.

For almost a year, Matthew refused to return to Phoenix because he wanted to immerse himself in the culture of his people. He wanted to talk with them, live with them, feel their pain and think like them. How else can you discover the needs of the people you're trying to reach? Phoenix was no longer his home; Los Angeles was.

MAKING A DIFFERENCE IN THE NEIGHBORHOOD

When he first arrived in Los Angeles, Matthew wasn't sure how he could affect the city, but he knew that God wasn't calling him to make a difference in the whole city yet. All he needed to do was make a difference in his neighborhood. And that he did.

Within eight months, nine hundred people were crowding into the building, and through services and various outreaches, five thousand were being touched each week. As we were faithful where we were, making a difference in our little world, God blessed us and enlarged it.

As of 1999, the Los Angeles International Church holds forty-two different services each week ministering to nine different ethnic churches, each with its own pastor and service in its own language. Plus we have twenty-seven different children's services. We have become one of the nation's fastest growing churches, reaching about thirty thousand a week.

OUR CIRCLE OF INFLUENCE

We never want to get away from the fact that God gives each person his or her own circle of influence—no matter how big or small. If we each make a difference in our particular world, together we will make a difference in *the* world.

One way my congregations apply this principle is through a program we call "Adopt-a-Block." To *adopt* means "to take in as one's own," and that's what we do. Each Saturday morning, a team of volunteers visits with the people in their block. Then they clean up the streets and help the residents by painting and cleaning their homes. They also provide clothing, food, baby-sitting, tutoring and lawn mowing. Most important, they share the love of Jesus. When people see that we are interested in truly helping them, their hearts are warmed to the gospel. Over time, we can't help but make a difference.

The Rampart division in Los Angeles county where the Dream Center is located has always been a very high crime district. But during our first three years there, the crime rate dropped 73 percent. This community used to be number one in car thefts in America. In 1998 they were thirtieth—in Los Angeles county! The mayor of Los Angeles recently gave us a commendation for making a difference in our community.

And that's how we're going to make a difference in Los Angeles—we're going to take the city one block at a time. You see, anybody can do that!

Your church may not be making a big impact on your city—yet. But if your people make an impact on a single block or a single neighborhood, eventually you will make an impact on your community, your city and perhaps even your country. As the old adage goes, "Despise not small beginnings."

God continues to enlarge our circle of influence in Phoenix as well. In 1999 we started a church in fashionable Scottsdale, Arizona. A man gave us $1 million in seed money to reach his community, and we began holding services in a 22,000-square-foot complex that seats twelve hundred. It's a beautiful structure encased in glass. Although the expenses were high, God provided the money we needed in order to reach the people of Scottsdale. In the first seven weeks over seven hundred attended.

Our people in Phoenix and Los Angeles believe God can do just about anything through them because they know they can make a difference in *their* world. And as they have proven themselves faithful, God has enlarged their world. In the parable of the talents, Jesus told the wise steward, "You were faithful over a few things, I will make you ruler over many things" (Matt. 25:21).

You Can Make a Difference in *Your* World

Something within each of us tells us we were born for adventure. God created us to do more than just enjoy life, live off the fat of the land and die. But the question remains, "How can I make a difference in my little world?" Here are some suggestions:

Pray. Ask God to show you where in your world you can make a difference. Jesus said, "Do you not say, 'Four months more and then the harvest'? I tell you, open your eyes and look at the fields! They are ripe for harvest" (John 4:35, NIV). Sometimes what we need most is for God to open our eyes so we can see the needs around us.

Find a need and fill it. Thousands are in bondage to perversion, material things, alcohol and drugs. People are dying from AIDS. Students are being killed in the schools, regardless of social strata. Your opportunities to make a difference are enormous. You don't have to tackle the biggest need—just find one and meet it with the love of Jesus Christ. Then you will find your circle of influence begin to enlarge.

Sacrifice. Give up your time, energy, money, pleasure, responsibility—perhaps even your reputation. God hasn't called us to spend our lives sitting on easy chairs watching television every evening. Nor has He called us to be constantly entertained.

I used to dream of being a good golfer. But I quit the game because it was unfair—they don't mow the grass where I hit the ball! I used to dream that someday I would live in the temperate climate of Flagstaff, Arizona, and play golf during the summers on my days off. We had even bought a lot there for our dream home. But then the Los Angeles adventure came, and I gave up the fairways for the freeways, the smell of pine trees for the scent of asphalt in the gang-ridden jungles of L.A. Sometimes we have to scrap a little dream for a big dream. But the big dream is the Pearl of Great Price—expensive, but worth the cost.

Be bold. You cannot hesitate to take the plunge. Plans remain just plans until they are carried out. Goals remain goals until they are achieved. The only failure is refusing to try.

Boldness may mean simply stepping out of your comfort zones. Or it may mean taking on responsibilities that require divine intervention to succeed. Just as every person is different, so is the measure of boldness God requires of each individual.

So, how do you make a difference in the world? Begin with a simple prayer like the one I prayed after chapel forty years ago: "God, I want to make a difference in *my* world."

God will honor your sincerity.

FOUR

For Such a
Time As This

*Who knows but that you have come to royal position for
such a time as this?*

—MORDECAI TO ESTHER

RECENTLY ON A flight to Los Angeles I sat next to a
sports announcer for NBC. We were acquainted because
our children had attended school together. A Christian,
he had even visited our church from time to time. He
asked me about the Dream Center, so I shared my vision
with him. Then I said, "You're a very successful
announcer. Why don't you tell me what your dream is?"

"Pastor Barnett," he began, "I'm living for the day when
I have that one defining moment. Every announcer wants
it—to be there when Mark McGwire hits his seventieth
home run or when somebody gets the hit that wins the
World Series. I long for that defining moment when I can

speak a word, say a sentence, explain what's happening in such a way that people will remember me forever. That is my dream."

RAISED UP FOR A PURPOSE

Do you yearn for your defining moment? I believe people want more than just fifteen minutes of fame. I believe they want that once-in-a-lifetime opportunity to make a difference.

The Bible tells the story of a young woman who was as unlikely as you or I to make a difference, and yet God used her. Despite being orphaned as a young girl and held captive in a foreign country, Esther was named queen of Persia, but she kept her Jewish heritage a secret from the king and his court.

During this time the king was tricked into signing an edict that allowed all the Jews of the kingdom to be exterminated. Esther was positioned as the only hope for the salvation of her people. Without Esther pleading on their behalf, the Jews would certainly perish.

In those days, going before the king without being summoned was risky. Unless King Xerxes officially recognized Esther as she entered his inner sanctum, she would be sentenced to death. The previous queen was removed from the throne due to her disrespect for the king. Esther too might be dethroned.

Though she recognized the great threat to her people, Esther debated with herself as to whether or not to appeal to the king on their behalf. So her uncle Mordecai sent these now famous words to her: "Who knows but that you have come to royal position *for such a time as this?*"

(Esther 4:14, NIV, emphasis added).

Esther chose to trust in God's divine providence. She went before the king, and he took her request to heart. The lives of countless Jews were spared. The courage of this young woman preserved the existence of the Jewish people, paving the way for the coming Messiah to be born of Jewish parents in Bethlehem five hundred years later.

PRINCIPLES FOR LIVING A LIFE OF PURPOSE

Four key principles from Esther's story shape the way I live my life and explain how God can use us to make a difference:

Principle #1: God has created each of us for a specific purpose.

All people are endowed with the seeds of greatness and the ability to rise above themselves to make a difference in the lives of others. God didn't create you just to watch football or to go to Disneyland. You weren't designed just to attend church on Sunday mornings. He created you to accomplish your life's purpose.

Discovering God's purpose for your life is what adventuring yourself is all about. We know intuitively when we are accomplishing our life's purpose because we enjoy what we are doing and we're good at it. No two people have the same combination of spiritual gifts, strengths and abilities. Because of this, no two people have the same purpose. Each individual's purpose was ordained by God to accomplish something special for the kingdom of God. That includes you.

The arenas in which people accomplish their purposes

vary in size. We recognize the names of Billy Graham and Mother Teresa because they have effectively carried out their purposes in a public arena. But a person need not be world famous in order to accomplish a purpose of equal importance to God.

In our church, I believe Dr. Donald Bogue was called by God to start our Pastors College. Lloyd Zeigler's purpose was to begin our Master's Commission program. I believe God created Larry Kerychuk to build a ministry to athletes. And I believe God raised up Tommy Barnett to pastor Phoenix First Assembly of God and to work with Matthew Barnett as a part of the L.A. International Church.

In the vast majority of cases, people perform their life purposes in the private arena. Some may lead a Bible study at work. Others may share their faith with neighbors or drive a bus route at church. But everybody has a life purpose.

Principle #2: Each of us is given an opportunity to change the course of the world.

I believe God has for each of us a "for such a time as this." A time—one time—in life when we can do something that will literally change the world.

You may think, *I'm not a world-changer. I'm just a housewife,* or maybe, *I just punch a time clock every morning.* But until she was named queen of Persia, Esther was just an orphan growing up in captivity in a strange country. She probably had no idea that something great would happen in her life. After becoming queen of Persia, perhaps she believed that was all God had for her. Her *purpose* may have been to rule as queen of Persia, but her *"for such a time as this"* was to save her people from total annihilation.

Your "for such a time as this" may come in the form of a

person. Esther was raised by her uncle Mordecai. Perhaps his life's purpose was to raise his niece to be a godly woman, and his "for such a time as this" was to influence her to go before the king. Or, your "for such a time as this" may come in the form of an event or an idea instead.

But whatever it is, you will have one.

My uncle, Ted Vazzer, was an Assemblies of God missionary in India for fourteen years. He ran an orphanage there, and he was faithful even though two of his own children died on the mission field because of the lack of available hospital care.

One day a runner came to Ted and said, "A man-eating leopard is terrorizing the village." Ted grabbed his shotgun and a few other supplies and went to help. Two boys named Benjamin Shindi and Solomon Wasker tried to follow him, but Ted gave them stern orders to stay. Nevertheless, they sneaked and followed him, wanting to be part of the adventure.

The way they caught leopards in that part of the world was to send hunters up the mountains to locate where the leopard came home to sleep. Leopards slept at the base of the mountains, and for some reason they would not go up the mountain, even when pursued. When the leopard was located, people from the village would beat the ground with sticks and bang tin cans together to scare it from its hiding place. As it ran around the mountain, hunters would be waiting to shoot it.

Ted and the villagers found this particular leopard and began chasing it around the mountain, but for some reason the leopard ran up the mountain. Unknown to anyone, Benjamin and Solomon were there watching the scene unfold. The leopard came directly at the boys and attacked them, grabbing Solomon by the leg. Solomon screamed, "Daddy!" Ted came over the hill and saw the animal clamped down on the boy's leg. Typically, leopards go for the leg to cripple their prey, then immediately lunge for the throat—and the kill.

Ted could hardly believe what he was seeing. As he watched the leopard hunch over his adopted son, he knew he was in a quandary. He had only a 12-gauge shot gun, the kind that sprays slugs powerful enough to kill a tiger. He couldn't shoot for fear of shooting both Solomon and the leopard. He couldn't get any closer, or the leopard would kill Solomon. As he watched, the leopard dropped the leg and made a motion toward Solomon's throat. Ted had no choice. He prayed and pulled the trigger. The shotgun sounded, and the bullets flew through the air. Ted watched as the leopard slumped over, dead. The boy had not been hit, but his leg was nearly severed.

They rushed Solomon to the hospital, miles away by truck, and the doctor said they would have to amputate the leg because of gangrene. The villagers asked for one day to pray for God's intervention, and as a result, God spared his leg. Ted's faith in confronting the leopard had saved the lives of Solomon and Benjamin.

Why do I tell this story? Because that day may have been Uncle Ted's "for such a time as this." Solomon went on to be the missionary who opened up to the gospel a huge unreached part of India called Nagaland. He interpreted for Billy Graham's crusades in India. He started hundreds of churches, many in places inaccessible by car. When people asked how he did it, he said, "I've got two good legs, and I'm going to use them for the glory of the Lord."

The other boy, Benjamin, became a leading teacher at

the Bible school in Bangalore and trained many godly men who are leading churches in India.

Principle #3: We don't know when our "for such a time as this" will come.

We each have a significant contribution to make to our generation. We have no idea what it will look like or when it will present itself. It may happen today. It may happen tomorrow. It may have already happened.

Uncle Ted did many great things during his time as a missionary, but only heaven will reveal to us what his "for such a time as this" was.

I don't know when my time will come, so I want to keep my life pure so I will not be judged unfit when my "for such a time as this" emerges. If my life isn't right with God, I may miss my opportunity altogether and not even know it.

I know pastors who could have been great, but they were lured away from their divine purpose by sexual perversion and lust. Others missed their "for such a time as this" because they could not be trusted with money. Some were just lazy.

If you fail, God can restore you and use you. Some of the greatest people used by God have failed miserably. But because no one knows when his or her time will come, even a brief foray into sin or nominal Christianity may mean the "for such a time as this" opportunity is missed.

Principle #4: We may not know what our "for such a time as this" was until we get to heaven.

I don't want to miss the "for such a time as this" for which God has placed me here on earth! So I must continue to be faithful in the little things in order that I will not be judged unqualified when the big things come. Which of those accomplishments in my life were really the "big" thing for which God created me? I probably won't know until I get to heaven. Therefore I must always be faithful to God's purposes for my life.

The apostle Paul lived from this perspective. He encouraged the church in Ephesus to "be very careful, then, how you live—not as unwise but as wise, *making the most of every opportunity,* because the days are evil" (Eph. 5:15–16, NIV, emphasis added). I must realize that every sermon is important, because I don't know if the next Billy Graham or Mother Teresa is in that service. On any given day, I may be brushing shoulders with royalty or greatness. Who knows?

But in order to avoid missing my "for such a time as this," I must position myself to be ready at any moment. I must be faithful to the particular ministry to which God has called me. I must keep my life clean, so that I can be ready for my "for such a time as this" and seize my defining moment.

Remember that little boy in John 6 who took his lunch box with him to hear Jesus preach? Suppose he had decided to stay home that day to watch Bozo the Clown on TV? I'm sure he had gone to "Sunday school" time and time again, but still he was sitting there that day in that crowd of five thousand people. Little did he know that was *his* day.

Andrew sat with the disciples. Little did he know when he went to "church" that Sunday morning that Jesus was about to feed five thousand people. Andrew was possibly the greatest children's worker in history. How can we tell?

You try taking a lunch bucket away from a hungry kid! That took somebody special. I can hear Andrew now saying, "Son, the preacher wants your lunch!"

Andrew was a plodder. He wasn't dynamic like his brother Peter. He wasn't favored as John was. He wasn't as well known as some of the others. But that day, he did something none of the others did: He convinced that little boy that Jesus needed his lunchbox. He did what those other men could not do. Now, two thousand years later, we're still talking about the time Jesus fed the five thousand. But without the little boy and Andrew, this miracle might not have happened. For this reason, we must remain poised for our "for such a time as this."

MY "FOR SUCH A TIME AS THIS" . . . ?

I have no idea when my "for such a time as this" will come. It may have occurred in Washington, D.C., when I preached at the National Black Pastors Conference. Since I was the only white guy preaching, I asked, "Why in the world would you invite me? I feel like the raven who is feeding the prophets." (See 1 Kings 17:4.) These black preachers were the greatest preachers in the world.

But the moderator of that meeting responded, "We chose you because you have a black heart." Well, that night I preached my "black" heart out as I spoke on "There's a Miracle in the House." Addressing the crowd, I distinctly remember saying that I had come that night looking for one person who would make a difference. I found him. I just didn't know it for awhile.

Ten years later T. D. Jakes invited me to preach at his first pastors' conference. Over seven thousand pastors filled the auditorium, and people were standing outside. "Brother Jakes, why did you invite me?" I had to know.

"Because ten years ago I was a struggling little pastor in North Carolina. I went to a pastor's conference in Washington, D.C., and you preached a message titled 'There's a Miracle in the House.' When you began to preach, something happened to me. And I said, 'God, if you just get me out of this place alive'—my heart was beating so fast—'I will be the miracle in the house.'

"I went home, my church began to grow and my ministry began to explode. I determined that because God used you to touch my life that night, if I ever had a pastors' school, I would invite you to be the opening night's speaker."

Today God is using T. D. Jakes to touch people around the world through his ministry as few others today are being used. Was that my "for such a time as this?" I don't know, but I'm glad I didn't turn down that speaking engagement because my schedule was too busy. I knew that I always needed to be available, so I didn't miss my "for such a time as this."

Or perhaps I witnessed my "for such a time as this" the Sunday morning when Sharon Henning, a layperson who volunteered in our wheelchair ministry, asked me, "What are we going to do? The person who heads up the wheelchair ministry just resigned."

"I want you to take it over."

"But I don't feel called," she objected.

"Until we get someone, take it over."

Six months later we still had no one to take her place. Once again, Sharon came to me. "Pastor Barnett, I just don't feel led to work the wheelchair ministry."

"Well, do it anyway until I get someone to do it," I consoled her. This time, I was determined to find someone because I knew she couldn't hold out much longer.

Soon thereafter she came to me with tears running down her cheeks. Expecting a repeat of our previous conversations, she surprised me, "Preacher, don't look for my replacement. God has called me to this work."

Eight years later, Sharon has become one of the foremost leaders in ministry to the physically challenged. She now has ten wheelchair buses picking people up for our church services, and she is a sought-after speaker at conventions around the world. The Lord raised her up for "such a time as this." Was that the big moment in my life? Perhaps.

Or perhaps I encountered my "for such a time as this" on the way to a church growth rally where I was speaking in Tucson, Arizona. At the airport I was greeted by the youth pastor who served as my host. This enthusiastic young man brought me to a nice motel and placed a beautiful basket of treats in my room. That night he conducted the service with poise and sensitivity like few I have ever seen.

By the end of the evening I was so impressed with his people skills and organizational abilities that I thought to myself, *I need someone like this on my staff. Maybe he'd be interested in working for me.* But then I came back to my senses. *I can't steal someone from a pastor who invited me to speak in his church. Besides, the pastor is this man's brother-in-law.*

The young man's name was Lloyd Zeigler. Although I didn't pursue any further discussions with this man, I kept his name tucked in the back of my mind.

Every year after that he came to our Pastors' School and applied the principles and ideas he had learned at his church. He literally became a Phoenix Assembly of God man in Tucson.

One day, a phone call was forwarded to my office. "Pastor Barnett, this is Lloyd Zeigler." It was so good to hear from him again. After sharing where God had brought us since we had seen each other last, he confided, "Pastor Barnett, I feel God's through with me here. I would love to work with you.

"Lloyd," the words were difficult to spit out. "I'd love to have you on my staff, but I just couldn't steal you away from your brother-in-law." He understood, but as I hung up the phone, I knew we were both disappointed.

A year later, Lloyd called me again. "Pastor Barnett, I believe God has impressed on me to move to Phoenix and get a job. I want to come to Phoenix First and prove myself to you, for I know that you raise up your staff from within your congregation. I believe God wants me to work with you."

That afternoon, Larry Kerychuk, the director of our sports ministry, called me, weeping. "Carmen Balsamo (the head of our Master's Commission) and I were jogging when he suffered a heart attack. I rushed him to the hospital, but I don't think he's going to make it." On the way to the hospital I knew Carmen was going to pass into the arms of Jesus that day. But as I drove, God clearly spoke to me, *It's no coincidence that after all these years, Lloyd called you this morning. He's the man for the Master's Commission.*

I called Lloyd's brother-in-law and received his blessing to bring him on our staff. Since his arrival, our Master's Commission has grown from a single ministry of our church to a national ministry of the Assemblies of God.

Lloyd Zeigler now leads from our church over one hundred Master's Commission groups around the world. Was that night I preached at the church growth conference in Tucson my "such a time as this"?

Or perhaps my "for such a time as this" involved my vision for the Dream Center. After accepting the invitation from Ray and George to expand into Los Angeles, I began to get cold feet. Originally I planned on making my first formal announcement concerning the Dream Center at our pastors' school that year and then taking an offering to get it started. But I had second thoughts and decided I wasn't going to California. *I don't want to do it. It's too great a task. And I'm not going to ask those pastors to give an offering to me.*

Just before the evening meeting was to begin, George Wood called unexpectedly. "I hear you're going to make the announcement and take up an offering for the Dream Center tonight. I want to be the first to give."

"Brother Wood," I reluctantly said, "I've decided I'm not going to go."

"Tommy, if you don't go to L.A., you will fall short of what God has called you to do, and you will miss the defining moment of your life. You will probably die a premature death, and you'll miss the moment for which God has put you here. You can't do that. This may very well be your 'for such a time as this.'"

Knowing that George was right, I went ahead and announced the beginning of the Dream Center at the Pastors' School. Who knows? That moment may have been George Wood's "for such a time as this."

Today, thirty thousand people a week are impacted through the ministry of the Dream Center—drug addicts, street people who live in boxes, AIDS patients, gang members, prostitutes and throwaway teenagers who live on Sunset Boulevard. The growth we have experienced is phenomenal! But best of all, Dream Centers are springing up all over America at a rate of almost one a week.

The Dream Center may be my "for such a time as this." But then again, it may not be. Maybe the time I spent raising my two sons, Matthew and Luke, was my "for such a time as this." God may have something even greater for me ahead.

People ask me, "Why do you keep pushing yourself? At your age, why do you keep piling more responsibilities on your plate?" Because I don't know if Jack Wallace was my "for such a time as this." Or Bill Wilson. Or the Dream Center. Or Phoenix Assembly of God. It may even be someone who is reading this book. I won't know until I get to heaven.

Suppose that young boy with the five loaves and two fishes would have stayed home…

Suppose Esther had been too scared to go before the king…

God has an appointment with you in the future, and the results could change the world. Where will you be when your "for such a time as this" comes?

FIVE

The Heart
of the Adventure

*It isn't what you wish to do, it's what you will do for God
that transforms your life.*

—HENRIETTA MEARS

DYING WORDS CAN offer a fascinating glimpse into a person's life. When a person approaches death, it seems they come closer to the heart of adventure than ever before. Their vision becomes clearer. They see what really matters—at least, some people do. Sometimes their last words sum up the kind of life they lived. Writer Joseph Addison, just before he died in 1719, said, "See in what peace a Christian can die." Legendary freak show creator P. T. Barnum's last words were, "How were the receipts today at Madison Square Garden?"

Ludwig van Beethoven reportedly said, "Friends applaud—the comedy is finished."

President Grover Cleveland's last words were, "I have tried so hard to do the right." Actress Joan Crawford is said to have scolded her housekeeper for praying, saying, "Don't you dare ask God to help me." Philosopher Voltaire, who spent his life antagonizing the church, was asked if he would forswear Satan, and he allegedly replied, "This is no time to make enemies."

Some have realized their powerlessness over life in their final moments. Elizabeth I, queen of England until 1603, said, "All my possessions for a moment of time." Another queen, Louise of Prussia, said in 1820, "I am a queen, but I have not the power to move my arms." Poet and horror story author Edgar Allan Poe said, "Lord, help my poor soul!"

Poet Heinrich Heine, as he lay dying, said, "God will pardon me. That's His trade." Leonardo da Vinci, painter of the Mona Lisa and one of history's unmatched inventors and artists, said, "I have offended God and mankind because my work did not reach the quality it should have." Mexican revolutionary Pancho Villa didn't plan his exiting words. "Don't let it end like this," he said as his life ebbed away. "Tell them I said something."

Karl Marx refused to leave last words for posterity. "Last words are for fools who haven't said enough," he remarked on his deathbed. Author William Saroyan, winner of the Pulitzer Prize, is said to have called his last words into the Associated Press: "Everybody has got to die, but I have always believed an exception would be made in my case. Now what?"

It's an interesting study. But I wonder, what do you want your last words on this earth to be?

LAST WORDS OF ETERNAL PROPORTIONS

I'll never forget a dear doctor from our church who was in his final hours. He had always been a blessing to me—he was an encourager, and he prayed for me often.

Moments before he passed into eternity I was at his side in the hospital room when he motioned for me to listen. His voice was already faltering, so I leaned closer in order to make out what he was saying.

"I'm just getting ready to take a trip I have been preparing to take for a long time. I am going to be with Abraham, Isaac and Jacob in the kingdom of God. Brother Tommy, is there anything that you want me to tell them when I get there?"

For the life of me, I couldn't think of anything. Then he said, "I'm going now. Put your ear down here." I put my ear next to his lips as he whispered words barely audible, yet still resounding within me to this day. "Preach it, Brother Tommy. Preach it, Brother Tommy."

Then suddenly, I heard the wings of angels and felt their breath as they hovered over that bed. One of the angels breathed quietly, "Please step out of the room. We have an assignment to carry out." As I left the room, they gathered the old man's spirit up and ushered him into glory.

Will I always remember what Doctor Haviland whispered to me in that hospital room? You bet. Do you think I'm going to "preach it?" Always.

The heart of the adventure is the gospel of Jesus Christ. Two thousand years ago, Jesus died and rose again. After spending forty days with His disciples, He prepared His followers for His ascension into heaven. Here were His parting instructions to the church:

"Go into all the world and preach the gospel to every creature. He who believes and is baptized will be saved; but he who does not believe will be condemned. And these signs will follow those who believe: In My name they will cast out demons; they will speak with new tongues; they will take up serpents; and if they drink anything deadly, it will by no means hurt them; they will lay hands on the sick, and they will recover."

So then, after the Lord had spoken to them, He was received up into heaven, and sat down at the right hand of God. And they went out and preached everywhere, the Lord working with them and confirming the word through the accompanying signs.

—MARK 16:15–20

If there is any validity in heeding a person's final words, then it behooves us to heed Jesus Christ's last words in even greater measure. And what was His final instruction? "Go." This command wasn't just for the twelve disciples, but for *every* disciple of Jesus Christ. Every believer is commissioned to go into all the world and preach the gospel to every creature.

The disciples' actions indicate that they must have understood the word *world* to mean "Jerusalem" because, despite Jesus' command in Acts 1:8 to go from Jerusalem into Judea, Samaria and the ends of the earth, they stayed there. But we can glean from the Book of Acts God's unrelenting determination for His church to obey Jesus' parting command to "go."

From our vantage point two thousand years later we can see how God permitted persecution as a means to drive the young believers out of Jerusalem and into the countryside. Luke describes the response of the church following to the stoning of Stephen, the first martyr: "On that day a great persecution broke out against the church at Jerusalem, and all except the apostles were scattered throughout *Judea* and *Samaria*" (Acts 8:1, NIV, emphasis added).

So the disciples went to Judea and Samaria, as Jesus had commanded. Later, Saul (renamed Paul after his Damascus experience), who instigated the persecution, was shortly converted to Christ. Then he obeyed Jesus' command to take the gospel to the *ends of the earth.* God doesn't leave business unfinished, no matter how reluctant we are!

SHARING THE GOSPEL—THE WORLD'S GREATEST ADVENTURE

Jesus' final command gives us four reasons why sharing the gospel is the greatest adventure of all.

Reason #1: We are sharing good news.

What were Jesus' final words? Basically the same as Dr. Haviland's: Preach the gospel. And what does *gospel* mean? Good News!

When I was a boy, I used to sneak into the empty church sanctuary where my father pastored and preach the varnish off the pews. One night while I was preaching, a man wandered in the back door, which somebody had left open. He looked around to see that no one else was in the church, then he sat down anyway and listened to me. He didn't mind and I didn't mind, so I kept on preaching.

When I came to the altar call, I said, "Everybody in this building, from the left to the right, from the front to the rear..." He looked around again. Nobody was there but him! "...when I get to the number three, if you want Jesus, run to the front. One...two..." When I got to "three," he stood up and ran to the front of the sanctuary. That man gave his life to Christ that very night!

People aren't going to be inclined to give their lives for something that comes across as "bad" news. I have seen plenty of people preach the gospel as if it were bad news. Their listeners rightly run away from such a false gospel. But when the world discovers we are bringing Good News, we will gain a hearing.

Reason #2: We offer hope of a changed life.

The gospel changes lives. In one word, the message of the gospel is "love." God loved us so much He sent His only Son, Jesus, to die on a lonely, splintered cross for our sins. In response we, the lost who have been found, love God with all that we have—hearts, minds, souls and strength. In gratitude for the love we experience, we then share the life-giving love of Jesus Christ with others. We don't force people to become Christians; we love them into the kingdom. We embody and share the Good News, and lives are changed by its power.

The Good News, then, is love in action. St. Francis once said, "Preach the gospel and, if necessary, use words."

Some say, "All you need to do is witness to people. Caring for the poor is for liberals." Other people believe their highest priority is to care for the underprivileged. Personally, I don't think the two should be separated. James encourages us:

What does it profit, my brethren, if someone says he has faith but does not have works? Can faith save him? If a brother or sister is naked and destitute of daily food, and one of you says to them, "Depart in peace, be warmed and filled," but you do not give them the things which are needed for the body, what does it profit? Thus also faith by itself, if it does not have works, is dead.

But someone will say, "You have faith, and I have works." Show me your faith without your works, and I will show you my faith by my works.

—JAMES 2:14–18

The key into a person's life is not through the head but through the heart—and sometimes through the stomach. Our acts of kindness, like God's, lead people to repentance (Rom. 2:4).

Reason #3: We are brokering in eternity.

Embarking on an adventure that involves eternity is high risk because the work lasts forever. Our actions—or the lack thereof—may mean the difference between heaven and hell for people. The salvation of even one man or woman results in the angels of heaven bursting into songs of joy.

Brokering in eternity means relying upon the power of God for our success. Embarking on the adventure means not only reading about examples such as those in this book—it means living them!

I made the first formal announcement of my involvement with the church in L.A. at a night meeting of our Pastors' School. Then I gave those present an opportunity to join me financially in this pursuit. But due to my ambivalence regarding the decision, I was ill-prepared to take an offering. No envelopes were ready, nor did I have pledge cards for people to fill out.

Nonetheless, I shared my vision that night and asked for any help those dear people could lend. All over the auditorium men and women from large, medium, small and fledgling churches were writing checks and scribbling on the backs of envelopes and other assorted pieces of paper. When the gifts were counted, the cash and pledges over a three-year period totaled an astounding $350,000! Following that meeting, money began pouring in from all over the nation.

The vision God gave me for the Los Angeles International Church was so big that it required divine intervention in order to pull it off. And that offering convinced me that I was moving ahead in God's timing and with God's blessing.

Seeing God intervene in our situations gives us the boldness to venture into new frontiers unrivaled even by the world's greatest adventurers. There is no life more exciting than the one that relies upon God to intervene.

Reason #4: We are building rewards in heaven.

Each of us is investing in the kingdom of God. What we allow God to work through us for the kingdom lives forever. And there is no greater purpose than to invest in the kingdom.

The apostle Paul encouraged his young protégé Timothy regarding his congregation:

> Command them to do good, to be rich in good

deeds, and to be generous and willing to share. In this way they will lay up treasure for themselves as a firm foundation for the coming age, so that they may take hold of the life that is truly life.

—1 Timothy 6:18–19, NIV

Some Christians live as if they expect to reside in low-income housing in heaven. They believe in Jesus and have accepted Him as their Savior, but they are lazy, self-concerned and disobedient. I know heaven won't have slums, but if it did, I wonder how many would find themselves spending eternity there?

As for me, I want palatial digs, in seventy-five degree weather, adjacent to the nicest golf course in heaven. Someday I want to bump into a man or woman on those streets of gold who will stop me and say, "Tommy, I want to thank you for walking across the desert to raise money for the Dream Center. If you hadn't done that, I wouldn't be here in eternity."

But most of all, I want to hear those sweet words of my heavenly Father: "Well done, my good and faithful servant."

The amount of time we spend here on earth is minuscule compared to the eons we will spend in glory. Investing in the kingdom of God is the only true, sound investment. All other returns on our investments remain here on earth.

The Stakes of a True Adventure

The goal of many adventure seekers is to see how close to death they can get and still return alive. Men and women who labor in the work of the kingdom not only venture close to the perimeter of hell, but they return with souls as well.

Recently when I was in Los Angeles, a person from the Dream Center showed me a video he had taped of a PBS program on television. Unbeknownst to me, a secular station visited the Dream Center to report on our ministry in the community.

The documentary shared the story and vision of the Dream Center. It explained how we obtained the old Queen of Angels hospital for a fraction of the asking price (that story is coming later). They interviewed a former prostitute who found Christ as the result of our prostitute ministry. At two o'clock one morning a person from our team had given her a rose and had shared with her the life-changing message of Jesus Christ. She accepted Christ, and her life was changed by the power of God. During her interview she commented, "No man, no organization could do this for me. Only the power of God."

They showed Billy Soto, a man with tattoos over much of his body who once played guitar in a rock-and-roll band. Billy's life had been nearly destroyed by a thirty-year addiction to heroin. During his downward slide, he lost his wife and precious children, but the Lord saved him. He's been serving the Lord now for over four years, and he is reunited with his wife and children. Now every week Billy delivers food to transients living under bridges as well as to people dying of AIDS.

I cried like a baby when I watched that program. It concluded with these comments: "This used to be a hospital that took care of the sick. But in a sense you could say that it is hospital now because it heals the spirit and the soul." And the closing words: "The Queen of Angels—the L.A. International Church—has made a difference."[1]

Kind words spoken not by an insider, but by a casual observer who saw what could happen when a group of people believe that the Good News of Jesus Christ does make a difference. And that, my friends, is the heart of the adventure we are on.

SIX

Is Your Adventure God's Adventure?

My great concern is not whether God is on our side; my great concern is to be on God's side.

—ABRAHAM LINCOLN

L ET ME ASK you a question: If you could do or be anything, regardless of talent, ability, education or cost, what would it be? The key to your answer may very well reveal the adventure God has in store for you.

In my experience I have found that most people cannot answer that question. They can tell you what they *don't* want in an adventure, but they cannot tell you what they *do* want. Once people remove the barriers from their minds, however, the sky is the limit in pursuing their adventure.

People often say to me, "Pastor, I would be willing to lay down my life and give everything I own if I could be certain that my adventure is God's adventure."

We know when we are pursuing God's adventure because somewhere in the midst of the pursuit, we discover a love for what we are doing. Our passions are drawn in, and the task ceases being tiresome.

When we pursue God's adventure, we find ourselves walking closer with Christ because we know the adventure can be accomplished only through Him. We naturally grow deeper in our faith, relying to a greater extent on God. We deal with sin issues because we want to please God, and we don't want to miss the opportunity for additional adventures.

When we pursue God's adventure, somewhere down the line we will see fruit because the adventure forces us to live in miracle territory. Lives will be changed. God's power will intervene.

FOUR TESTS TO TAKE BEFORE DIVING INTO AN ADVENTURE

Ideas are a dime a dozen. There are ideas, and then there are adventures born from the heart of God. At Phoenix First Assembly, before beginning a new adventure, we run every idea through four tests.

Test #1: Is anybody else doing it?

We're not interested in reinventing the wheel. If other ministries are already operating in this area—even if they exist outside our church or denomination—we work to cooperate with them. At best we join forces with them, and at the least we learn from them.

Test #2: Is there a need?

We believe in the old adage that the secret to success is finding a need and filling it. If the ministry doesn't scratch where people itch, we may postpone it until a later date when it does meet a need.

Test #3: Does it heal hurts or alleviate suffering?

Jesus revealed the Father's heart through the works He did among the people. When we heal hurts or alleviate suffering, we communicate to people that the needs of every person matter to God.

Test #4: Will it lead people to Jesus Christ?

If in the end our actions neither draw people closer to Christ nor lead them to salvation, then our efforts are futile. All we are doing is delaying an eventual hell.

One question we never ask is, *Can we afford it?* If God is calling us to a specific adventure, He will supply the resources needed for its accomplishment. It is our experience that money follows ministry.

FOUR QUESTIONS TO IDENTIFY WHETHER THE ADVENTURE COMES FROM YOU OR FROM GOD

How do you know whether the adventure comes from you or from God?

Question #1: Is this adventure bigger than you?

If you can pull it off on your own, it isn't God's adventure. A true adventure from God will take you through the heart of miracle territory. Paul reminds us that God is "able to do exceedingly abundantly above all that we ask or think, according to the power that works in us" (Eph. 3:20). Fortunately God isn't limited by the limitations we place on Him.

Could I have raised $4 million for the Dream Center on my own? No. If we can accomplish the adventure on our own, then we don't need God, and He won't get the glory. In the spiritual world, we are called upon to attempt things so big that everybody knows that if the dream comes to pass, it has to be God. Otherwise, we will fall on our faces.

Question #2: Do you hold the adventure, or does the adventure hold you?

Anyone can conjure up an exciting adventure. Coming up with an adventure isn't the problem—sustaining the dream for its accomplishment is.

As I said before, I believe if you can hang on to a dream for five years, it will come to pass. Along the way, discouragement, critics and naysayers will try to derail it. If you hold on to the adventure, eventually you'll lose strength and let go. But if the adventure comes from God, it will hold you, and you won't be able to escape its grip. When you go to bed, you'll think about it. When you wake up in the morning, you'll think about it. Finally you'll say, "I can't take it any longer! I won't rest until it is completed!"

Question #3: Are you willing to give your life to the adventure?

Halfhearted attempts at accomplishing the adventure usually end up causing heartache. Football players resent playing with teammates who give only lukewarm effort, because the slacker exposes the entire team to injury when he misses an assignment. So the question really is: Are you willing to do what it takes to see the adventure brought to completion?

Question #4: Are you willing to die for the adventure?

This is the all important question. People tell me, "Pastor Barnett, you're going to kill yourself. You don't take any time off. You're pastoring four churches now. This is going to send you to an early grave."

But I respond, "Because I know this is God's dream, I would gladly die to see this dream fulfilled."

When God plants the seeds of an adventure in our hearts, nothing will move us. A man dying of AIDS once pointed a gun at Matthew's head and said, "People don't care about AIDS victims, so I'm going to kill you and then kill myself. Together it will bring attention to AIDS and to the Dream Center."

Fortunately, God miraculously delivered Matthew from the man. But did the situation deter Matthew from moving ahead? Not on your life!

FEAR IS CONQUERED AT THE CROSS

Fear prevents people from dying for the adventure: fear of suffering, fear of death, fear of the unknown.

Overcoming fear requires that we go to the cross. That is the place where not only Jesus died, but where we also die to our own ambitions, greed and desires. When we have laid our own desires at the cross, then we can ask anything in His name, and He will give it to us.

Jesus said, "If you abide in Me, and My words abide in

you, you will ask what you desire, and it shall be done for you" (John 15:7). People assume Jesus' promise applies to everybody, but it doesn't. It only applies to people who abide in Christ—people who deny themselves and lay down their lives at the cross. Then you can ask for anything you want. I believe that with all my heart.

Recently I announced to our congregation that due to an ongoing building project and the normal downturn in giving during the summer months, our projections for the next ninety days showed we would run below budget. We asked God to bless our finances, and then I issued a challenge: "For all of you people who are not tithing, I ask that you just prove God for the next ninety days this summer, and see what He does when you walk by faith and tithe."

Following the service, a man walked up to me with a check in his hand and said, "I already gave a million dollars last year, but the Lord impressed upon me to try and give a million dollars every year. Use this for the budget this summer." And he handed me a check for $100,000!

That same day after church I went out to eat with a man from California who loves the Dream Center. We discussed the financial struggles we were having at the time trying to meet all the codes required by Los Angeles city regulations. At the end of our meal, the man said, "I have something for you. I received a big bonus that I was going to invest, but God told me the Dream Center needs it." Then he also handed me a check for $100,000.

To be honest, I was completely humbled. I have denied myself things like vacations and free time. I travel around the world and preach every week, not keeping any money so that every last penny can go to the Dream Center. I have given my life to the Dream Center, and I am willing to die in order to see its ministry continue. Over the last four years it cost me a fortune—but it has been the most productive four years of my life.

And now I believe that I can ask God for anything for His work and I will get it—because I have met those conditions. Listen to Jesus' words:

> Whoever desires to come after Me, let him deny himself, and take up his cross, and follow Me. For whoever desires to save his life will lose it, but whoever loses his life for My sake and the gospel's will save it.
>
> —MARK 8:34–35

When my focus is on God's adventure, He will supply the needs in order to see *His* adventure succeed.

SEVEN

The Adventure of Giving All

Those who turn back know only the ordeal, but they who persevere remember the adventure.

—MILO L. ARNOLD

THE BUSTLE OF Calcutta swirled around us we drove through the city. Through the car window I could see blind and lame beggars, women in colorful saris and vendors selling vegetables from wooden carts. Cows walked leisurely in and out of traffic, untouchable because the Indians consider them sacred.

"O Jesus, Jesus, help me," came the voice beside me. It was Mark Buntain, driving and rocking back and forth as he prayed to God. I was a young evangelist in my twenties visiting him as I traveled around the world holding revival meetings. I did not know it, but he was at a crisis point in his life. As we continued on, Mark seemed to fall apart.

"Jesus, O Jesus, what am I going to do?" he said, almost oblivious at times to my presence. Finally he pulled over and started crying. Tears coursed down his face. Then he turned to me and said, "Tommy, pray for me. I'm having a nervous breakdown."

"Brother Mark, I will pray for you, but you need to get away and go back to America. Take a break from all this."

"I can't," he said. "It's so difficult for Americans to get back into India. I can't abandon the work here."

After a moment I prayed that God would come along-side and help him complete the task he had been given, and that he would have renewed faith and joy. I did not know it then, but years later Mark would write about how, in that moment, it felt as if a band lifted from around his head. God healed him right in the middle of that trying emotional situation.

A true adventure demands that we push ourselves to the limit and draw upon our last reserves in order to see the goal accomplished. There is no going halfway with God. It will demand everything you have and much that you don't. I am reminded of another story that took place on August 3, a hot, muggy evening, at the 1992 Olympics in Barcelona, Spain.

The competitors aligned themselves on the starting line, knowing that in a few brief seconds, only the three runners with the fastest times would qualify for the 400-meter finals a few days away. Focusing on the goal in front of them, the runners listened for the sound of the starting gun.

When they heard the familiar "pop," they sprinted toward the finish line. A quarter of the way into the race, one runner, Britain's Derek Redmond, crumbled to the rubber pavement clutching his leg. He had torn a hamstring.

Medical attendants rushed onto the track to assist Redmond, but they were rebuffed by the obviously injured but still resolute runner. Though the rest of the runners had finished the race, Redmond struggled to his feet, grasped his leg and hobbled toward the finish line.

Four years earlier Redmond had qualified for the 1988 Olympics in Seoul, Korea. Ninety seconds before his heat he had to withdraw because of Achilles tendon problems. After five successive surgeries, he managed to qualify for this Olympiad, only to be blindsided by this career-ending injury.

But he said to himself, *I'm not quitting. I'm going to finish this race.* On a lonely stage before millions, Redmond slowly limped down his lane.

A big man barreled out of the stands, hurled aside a security guard, ran to Derek's side and embraced him. He was Jim Redmond, Derek's father. Arm in arm, they lumbered down the track together. Derek buried his face in his father's shoulder in grief and pain. The crowd, now aware of what was happening, stood to their feet and cheered until Derek and his father finally crossed the finish line.[1]

What an awesome description of our heavenly Father's help in our pursuit of the dream. In reality, no one is able to complete the adventure without the strong arm of the Lord. Not me, not you, not Mark Buntain, not Derek Redmond.

Pursuing an adventure exacts a price, and not everyone will live the unique adventure God has for them. For some, the price will seem too great. Someone once said, "The greatness of a person is measured by the size of one's dream and the price one is willing to pay in order to see it accomplished."

ADVENTURE YOURSELF

The Price of the Great Adventure

Every adventurer must give his or her all. Professional athletes pay a price to compete at their level of skill. When a baseball player fails to run out a ground ball or a basketball player walks instead of runs down the court, he risks getting benched. In pursuing the adventure, there must be a sense of reckless abandon, an attitude that says, "It's better to ask for forgiveness than to ask for permission." The mind-set of an adventurer is one of complete and utter dedication.

Often the difference between failure and success is not ability, but commitment to the purpose.

Climbing Mt. Everest will cost you $30,000 to $50,000—a steep price to put your life on the line. But embarking on an adventure for the kingdom of God costs even more.

In Mark 10 we find the account of Jesus encountering a rich, young ruler. The man must have been earnest in his desire, because he ran to Jesus, fell on his knees and asked, "What must I do to inherit eternal life?" He sincerely wanted to know the way.

Jesus told him to obey the commandments. The man then interrupted Jesus, essentially saying, "I have done that since I was a boy, but still there is something missing."

So Jesus took him one step further and told him to sell everything and give it to the poor. Then, Jesus said, "Take up the cross, and follow Me" (v. 21).

Pushed beyond the limits of what he was willing to give, the young man walked away. Unfortunately, he would never know the eternal riches he was forfeiting by hanging onto the things of this world.

Some people believe Jesus was merely testing him, just

trying to find out if the man was willing to sell everything. They say that if he had been willing, Jesus would not have required it of him. I don't believe that. I don't believe Jesus plays games with us. If the young man had said, "OK, I'll sell everything I have," I believe that Jesus would have told him, "Great. I'll just wait for you to liquidate everything and give it to the poor. Then when you return, you can join us. We'll be on our way, and together we'll rely on God to provide for our needs."

That kind of a response is not out of the realm of possibilities. When Jesus sent His followers out two by two, they were instructed not to take *anything* with them—including money (Luke 10:4).

How Much Is Your All?

Years ago I visited the starting point of the Mississippi River in Minnesota. I was amazed at how such a great river begins as such a small trickle. This poor excuse for a stream is so narrow you can jump across it. At the headwaters of the Mississippi, no power plants are stationed to siphon off the power of the river. No industries depend upon that small stream. But if you follow the river to its end at the delta at New Orleans, it stretches as far as the eye can see.

Whether you're jumping over that little brook in Minnesota or water skiing across it in Louisiana, it is still the Mississippi River. A river is the same river from the headwaters where it begins to the mouth where it feeds into the ocean.

The work of God in us is much like that river. When the life-giving river of God breaks forth into our lives, it resembles a little stream. God wants us to start as a trickle. But as we mature He wants that river to get bigger and wider until it grows into an exciting, adventurous delta that gives life to everything it touches. God wants us to end strong like the mighty Mississippi!

When my daughter, Kristie, was a little girl, she would bring me pictures she had drawn in Sunday school. Some of them were of a very skinny man with purple hair. I remember asking her, "Who is that?"

"Daddy, can't you recognize who that is? That's you," she explained.

Then, like most loving fathers, I would say, "That's a lovely picture."

But if Kristie were to come to me now with the same kind of picture, I would say to her, "That was OK when you were small, but I expect something better out of you now."

I'm concerned that in our Christian walk, we too often do just that. We are saved, we are accepted, we are justified, we are His—and we state, "I want to stay right where I am." But God says, "Grow up. It's time you moved down the river."

God never requires of us more than what we are able to give. But He does require of us *all* we are able to give. The all you had yesterday is not the all you have today, and what your all looks like today is not what your all will look like tomorrow. The level of maturity I expected from Kristie as a girl is different from the level of maturity I expect from her today.

My God expects much more of me today than He expected of me five years ago. In fact, as we are faithful in giving Him our all, He enlarges it, and then He asks us to give even more. But remember, the rewards of giving Him our all make life an adventure.

We sing, "All to Jesus I surrender, all to Him I freely give,"[2] but we want to sing that song once and for all, and that's it. We think our "all" means our life of sin before we got saved. But that is only the beginning of a lifetime of giving our all to Jesus.

ALL FOR THE SAKE OF THE DREAM CENTER

Shouldering the responsibility for the Dream Center has been one of the greatest faith stretches I have ever experienced. It has required more than I thought I could give. But as I gave, I found I had even more to give. There is no adventure worth having that doesn't require my all.

Seeing the Dream Center come to fruition required singular focus and dogged determination. One of my greatest concerns in September 1994 involved our facility. Bethel Temple was the church they offered me, but with a seating capacity of only one thousand people, it seemed too small for what we were pursuing.

So before the work in L.A. began, George Wood and I looked at many available buildings. The historic Ambassador Hotel was right downtown on Wilshire Boulevard. It was the place where Robert Kennedy was assassinated as well as the home of the Copacabana nightclub, which was owned by Donald Trump. We pursued those options, but they didn't pan out.

As the clock continued to tick and money kept coming in, I grew restless regarding a facility. The project was taking on a life of its own. We continued our search. The Lawry Seasoning Company had seventeen acres right next to Dodger Stadium. It was gorgeous, resembling a small Knott's Berry Farm. However, we were halted again—this time by a political figure who was not in favor of the sale because he had other plans. My heart sank—again.

Other buildings offered great potential, but one by one, God closed the doors. I felt like Derek Redmond on the track. My only hope was that my heavenly Father would come to pick me up and carry me across the finish line. Had I not been willing to give my all and focus on the goal, I doubt the project would have ever taken off.

Reminded that we should not despise the day of small beginnings, I thought about Bethel Temple again. I wrestled with the fact that once we began our program, it would fill up quickly. Then what? Yet the initial invitation Ray Rachel and George Wood had extended to me was to pastor Bethel Temple. Soon, square one—Bethel Temple—was the only square on the horizon, so I made the decision to start right there.

Bethel Temple may have appeared a far cry from the optimum facility, but it was available. And the precious people who faithfully remained in attendance had prayed for years that revival would move into their church. Their fervent prayers were being answered!

I carefully scheduled my time between Phoenix and Los Angeles. We sought our Master's Commission people to help us prepare the ground and start ministering in the neighborhood. This splendidly trained group of young people moved into the inner city.

At the first Saturday night youth rally, Bethel Temple was full for the first time in twenty-five years! So were our hearts.

I had made the commitment to give my all, and I have never looked back.

TRADING IN THE TEMPORAL FOR THE ETERNAL

It had always been my desire to spend my latter years living on a golf course. Right about this time, Marja and I were just days away from building our dream home in Flagstaff, Arizona, on property right next to a lovely golf course. As the day approached to make the transaction, we both knew we could not follow through with it. We subsequently sold the lot in Flagstaff and rented an apartment in downtown Los Angeles.

Somehow, that transaction is strangely reminiscent of the rich, young ruler. We are told that he walked away sad. Why would he walk away sad? After all, he didn't give his things to the poor. Conventional wisdom says you're sad if you *lose* your possessions, not keep them. But the rich, young ruler was sad because he was unable to let go of what he had. In reality, he didn't own his possessions. His possessions owned him. He had forfeited the great dream of his life, and he knew it.

Had the rich, young ruler given his all to Jesus, he would have found what he was searching for and his adventure would have just begun.

Scripture tells us we have to give God all we have in order to receive what God has for us. We have to let go of the old to get the new. We have to let go of old hurts and old relationships that have turned bitter in our mouths. Sometimes we have to let go of the good to get the very best. You see, the enemy of the best is the good, because something about us says, "I'm not going to let go of this until God shows me something better."

Giving all to God is the foundational character quality of the adventurer. If our all isn't on the altar every day, then when things don't go according to plan, the temptation is great to lie there on the track and wait for medical personnel to carry us to the sidelines. Then we never cross the finish line.

LOSING YOUR LIFE TO GAIN IT

Living the adventure requires complete focus on the goal and utter self-denial. This discipline results in gratification down the road. When Derek Redmond was splayed out on the track and racked with pain, he had to focus on the finish line while at the same time denying himself.

That's the irony of pursuing the dream, of embarking on the adventure: We set a goal, and then we abandon ourselves completely in order to see it achieved. We give Him our all, then God blesses us with even more so we can turn around and give it back to Him again.

The greatest adventurer in the history of the church, Paul, brings his perspective to giving his all:

> I have become all things to all men so that by all possible means I might save some. I do all this for the sake of the gospel, that I may share in its blessings. Do you not know that in a race all the runners run, but only one gets the prize? Run in such a way as to get the prize.
>
> —1 CORINTHIANS 9:22–24, NIV

EIGHT

The Adventure of Taking Risks

No noble thing can be done without risks.

—MONTAIGNE

A RECENT ISSUE OF *National Geographic Adventure* magazine listed what it called the twenty-five greatest adventures in the world, available to thrill seekers for a price. Among them:

- Searching for lost tribes in the forests of New Guinea where reportedly people still practice head-hunting and cannibalism.
- Hunting with nomadic peoples in Mongolia who use golden eagles to catch rabbits, foxes and wolves.
- Scuba diving in an underwater cave in Mexico's Yucatan jungle.

ADVENTURE YOURSELF

- Kayaking in grizzly bear country in the Yukon. [1]

Even as a lifelong risk-taker, I recognize that some of these tread the line between adventure and stupidity. You have to know what risks are good and what risks are bad. Failure to know the difference could cost you your life.

Marja and I were married on a Saturday, and we embarked on a rather unusual honeymoon. First we went to church the next Sunday morning at my father's church in Kansas City. Then we flew to the Philippines where I was going to hold meetings. The missionaries met us at the airport—and how impressed they were with my beautiful Swedish wife! We stayed in the missionary's guest bedroom upstairs, and every morning they woke us up at 5 A.M. for breakfast.

We held an outdoor revival there, and thousands came. Then we flew to India to hold meetings in a soccer stadium, but a typhoon destroyed the stadium. The missionary, gracious as he was, said, "It's your honeymoon, and I want to help you." He gave us a car, a driver and a cook and sent us to a maharaja's compound in a game preserve in the jungle. We stayed there, all by ourselves, for one week, and virtually the whole time was spent prowling the jungles hunting wild animals. Every night we got into an oxcart and drove into the jungle and saw every kind of animal we could imagine. Our guides handed me a gun, and though I have never been a hunter, I became one that week. After all, I was twenty-one years old and had a bride to impress!

One day we were out hunting and a jungle goat ran by, chased by a jungle dog. They disappeared, and I heard the goat cry out. I ran over the hill and saw the dog starting to clamp down on the goat's legs, so in a fit of compassion I shot the dog to try to save the goat. The goat was already dying, so I was forced to shoot it, too.

The next day a sambar, an elk-like creature, lifted its majestic head up out of the foliage as we passed by. I had never seen anything like it. The grace and beauty of that animal took my breath away, so I was secretly glad when I aimed—and missed. The guides were disgusted with me because they would have shared in the bounty, as was the custom. The next day we saw another sambar, and with this one, I got a lucky shot. Marja had to sit on the dead animal all the way back to the compound as the guides sang my praises. In one day I went from being the worst to the best hunter they had ever seen. That night, all the village came and feasted on the sambar. Only then did I feel good about shooting the beautiful creature.

On the last day, we were going through the jungle at dusk and Marja nudged me. "Look!" she whispered. I turned my head and saw a tiger with orange, white and black stripes, sitting very quietly. The guide was so frightened that he was shaking. I remembered what the missionary had said: "When you shoot a tiger, shoot it again and again because a tiger can run one hundred yards in four seconds. If you don't stop it, it'll be on you before you know it." I quietly lifted the rifle to my shoulder, aimed and pulled the trigger.

To my great relief the tiger rolled over. "Don't shoot again!" said our guide. "I want to tell everyone you got him with one shot." Foolishly, I took his advice and began walking toward the tiger when suddenly the tiger leapt up and disappeared into the bushes. I could hear him growling at me from somewhere nearby. We hurried back to the village, and the next day we retraced our steps but could not find the tiger. A week later, after I was gone, the vultures began to circle, and the guides were able to find the beautiful beast. I had wounded it, and it had died later. They tanned the hide and sent it to me as a trophy, and from what I understand, they closed the jungle after that. It was the last tiger to be taken out of that part of the country.

I don't think I would go hunting for tigers today, even if it were legal. I have too much love for animals, and I don't enjoy killing for sport. But even more, I have a healthy respect for my own life. I believe God gave us that wonderful honeymoon, and I wouldn't change a day of it. But I would be wary today of venturing into a jungle in pursuit of dangerous animals, unless God specifically told me to do so. I have learned over the years how to distinguish between good risks and bad risks. I am very interested in taking good risks. I am not interested in taking bad ones.

Risk as a result of obeying God is always good. I knew Los Angeles was dangerous before we went there. I knew I was willing to give my life for the church, but risking my son Matthew's life was a different story. He would be living in a volatile, dangerous area and encountering dangerous people. Obedience, not safety, would be the priority. For a while, I was afraid it was too great a risk. I became aware, though, that God was requiring it of us and that he too must be placed on the altar.

Fears such as this can prevent an adventure from even beginning. Faith fostered in the presence of God is the antidote to fear. But how do we know when the risk is too great? How can we tell a good risk from a bad risk? Although the two may look similar, a fatal chasm exists between them.

REACHING FOR THE HIGHEST COMES WITH RISK

When I was a child we used to sing an old schoolyard rhyme. A line from it went something like this:

> The higher up the cherry tree,
> the sweeter grow the cherries.
> The more you hug and kiss a girl,
> the more she wants to marry.

The risk in reaching for the very best cherries at the top of the tree is that you may fall out and injure yourself. The risk of hugging and kissing a girl is that she may want to get married. How do you know which risk is worthwhile? How do you know which adventure is a good risk and which is a bad one?

All adventures are not created equal. Let me tell you about a young man who stood on the top of a high ledge and looked down over a river. His friends, one by one, jumped in feet first. Everybody shouted with glee as they cannonballed into that river.

The young man decided to go head first. Some said, "No, you'd better not do it. You might get hurt." Others said, "You're too chicken to do that." Still others said, "Go ahead." This young man declared, "I'm not afraid," and dove in head first. When he went under the water, he struck his head against the bottom, severed his spine and spent the rest of his life paralyzed, confined to a wheelchair. That was a bad risk.

Now let me tell you about another man. Ed was a school teacher who attended our church. One day he said to himself, *I'm going to take a risk. I am going to live an adventurous life because I believe that there is more out there that what I'm doing.*

Without any experience, he became a builder. Today he is tremendously successful in Phoenix. God has blessed him, and he has helped advance the kingdom of God with his resources. That was a good risk.

SEVEN CRISIS POINTS IN RISK TAKING

How can you tell the difference between a good risk and a bad risk? My friend Mark Rutland recently named seven crisis points in deciding between a good and a bad risk. The success or failure of any adventure revolves around these points.[2]

Crisis Point #1: Addiction to thrills

Do you confuse the addiction to thrills and adrenaline with the true, wonderful joy of spiritual adventure? Some people take risks simply because they enjoy the adrenaline high or the attention. The young man who dove into the river and paralyzed himself wanted the excitement, the thrill and the ego gratification of having everybody say, "Look how brave he is." But it didn't turn out that way.

The problem with addiction to thrills is that a greater and greater level of thrill is needed to sustain the anticipated rush of adrenaline. Ask yourself these questions: *Why am I doing this? What is my true motivation? Is this simply a thrill-seeking mechanism, or is it an adventure truly directed by God?*

Often, even subconsciously, our ventures can be attempts to impress others. *If I join the street witnessing team, people will think I'm really bold.* Pastors can be just as guilty of wrong motives as laypeople. Although God can still use people like this (how many of us have completely pure motives?), our greatest rewards come when we do things for the right reasons.

Crisis Point #2: Unresolved regrets

A regret is a disappointment from a previous experience, something you wish had turned out differently. Do you have regrets from the past that are still not reconciled?

Many people live emotionally and spiritually paralyzed because of missed opportunities from the past. Perhaps they believe they missed their "for such a time as this" and have never been the same since. Most of us have had that feeling at some point in our lives. It is nothing to be embarrassed about. But problems arise when we leave this tension unresolved.

People with unresolved regrets respond to risks in different ways. First of all, they can become overly cautious and fatalistic about taking any risks at all. Because their missed opportunity is unresolved, they quit participating in the business of living. Life now happens *to* them instead of *through* them. They do not choose, they do not dare, they do not decide—they do not risk.

The second way people respond to unresolved regrets is by perceiving themselves as victims of their circumstances. Their unresolved regrets result in increased levels of anger when they face other risks.

More than one man has angrily confessed to me, "I wanted to go to the mission field, but I couldn't go because my wife wouldn't go with me." He then directs his anger at his wife. Instead of the risk energizing him, it depresses him and makes him angry. The very stimulus that could make him a better person makes him angry at others.

I have made some first-class mistakes in my life, but I refuse to allow the regret of the risk not taken in the past to paralyze me. I refuse to be angry at myself and others, and I will not live as a victim instead of living in victory.

The only way to deal with our unresolved regrets is to lay them down at the foot of the cross and allow God to cleanse us from the past. Then we can move forward into the future without taking indecision and anger with us.

Crisis Point #3: Expectation of perfection

Are your expectations unrealistic? Many people in their thirties struggle with this. They put off taking risks because they want the perfect environment. They're waiting to buy that perfect computer or television because they know it's going to get better and cheaper. They sit posed on the edge of their couch with the remote control, waiting for life to happen for them on the screen.

Had I waited for the perfect situation in order to venture into Los Angeles, I would still be waiting today! Everything in life has trade-offs. There is no path devoid of risk. Roses have thorns, and thorns have roses. With more victories will come more problems. I have more problems today than I have ever had in my life. But I also have more victories.

So, you add up the trade-offs and then make the best decision you can. Theodore Roosevelt once said:

> Far better is it to dare mighty things, to win glorious triumphs, even though checkered by failure, than to rank with those poor spirits who neither enjoy much

nor suffer much, because they live in the gray twilight that knows not victory or defeat.[3]

Crisis Point #4: Clinging to past adventures

Are you basing your decisions on past experiences? It's human nature to glorify the past. We like to remember the "good old days," forgetting that when we were living in the "good old days," we failed to recognize them as such. Rarely do we realize the value of the moment until it is only a memory. Over time, our tendency is to become a prisoner of the past. We fail to grasp that, as old adventures die, new adventures rise up to take their places. They in turn die and give way to new adventures once again.

There is no future in the past. God is not in the past, nor is He in the future. He is in the now. God is constantly moving us higher, farther and deeper. The Bible says that God takes us from glory to glory (2 Cor. 3:18).

Jesus told the church in Ephesus that they had left their first love. (See Revelation 2:4.) Countless people live on old experiences and yearn to get the tingle back that they first had when they were saved. They long for the old songs, the sermons they used to hear, the move of the Spirit they remember.

But the measure of our maturity is not based upon our ability to replicate past experiences. Anybody can enjoy the trip the first time, but character and commitment are required to return year after year. All too often we beat our brains out trying to get back our first love experience, when what we really need is to embrace the adventure of moving on in spiritual maturity and commitment.

Furthermore, God does not call us to repeat the experiences of the past. God spoke through the prophet Isaiah,

"Behold, I will do a new thing" (Isa. 43:19).

Have you limited God to moving only within the realm of past experiences?

Crisis Point #5: Not realizing what is at risk

Do I realize all who will be affected by the risk I take? Society today tells us to do what is best for us. But is that the best way?

When a single young woman decides to enter into an unholy, sexual relationship with the person she loves, she often justifies it by saying, "What we do behind closed doors doesn't affect anyone else but us." But she may be risking her own life and the life of a potential child. Plus, if she does become pregnant, the lives of her parents and her grandparents will probably be affected as well. She is also risking her testimony and the wrath of God, and ultimately, she is risking eternity. Yet she is completely out of touch with what is at risk.

We need to realize that the decisions we make rarely affect only us. Decisions made by the parents affect children. We should never risk the spiritual and eternal for what is fleeting.

Crisis Point #6: Failing to weigh sufficiently the positives against the negatives

Have you taken inventory of the costs and benefits surrounding the risk? One couple says, "Rather than risk exposing any more innocent children to such a wicked, godless society, we have decided not to have any kids." Unfortunately, this couple may not have sufficiently analyzed the possible losses against the possible gains.

Children bring additional problems, fears, anxieties and

sometimes grief. They will disappoint us and break our hearts. Plus, they're expensive! But they also bring tremendous gains. Couples who forego having children never know the joy of holding a little baby—their own flesh and blood—in their arms. They miss the joy of watching their children explore the new world around them. Plus, they miss out on the opportunity for God to use their children to work in their lives as well. In my opinion, a godly investment into the life of a child in the long run pays much greater returns than having no children at all.

We all face similar dilemmas in the risks we take. A wife says, "I'm afraid that if I forgive my husband, he'll just take advantage of me again. The only way I can prevent him from hurting me again is by holding an emotional debt over his head." But she fails to understand the benefits that could be hers by running the risk of forgiveness. The return on forgiveness is healing, power, love, deliverance, romance, joy and liberty.

A man once asked me to pray for his son's salvation, so I asked, "Why don't you invite him to church?"

"I'm afraid to," he replied. "My son might say no, and I'm not good at handling rejection." The man wasn't willing to run the risk of being rejected, so he didn't invite his son to church. He missed out on the potential return of eternal life for his son.

Churches can make the same mistake. In order to pacify a small contingent a pastor may keep from rocking the boat instead of daring to explore new methods of sharing the gospel. Many a congregation has died on the vine because it wasn't willing to take the risk of changing and maturing.

Crisis Point #7: Failing to understanding the risk ladder

Have I had success with previous risks I've taken?

When I left the church in Davenport, Iowa, we were the fastest-growing church in the nation. The Lord had literally given us that city. But as I mentioned before, one day God impressed upon me to go to Phoenix, Arizona.

After making my announcement, some people advised me, "A man only does a great work in one city. God gives him an anointing for that city, and if he leaves, he will lose the anointing of God. It never happens twice in a person's lifetime." A precedent had been established within my denomination that if a man was successful in a particular church, God was calling him to remain in that church the rest of his life.

But I had learned not to be content with doing ministry the way other men had always done it. I discovered that if people would not come to me, then I should to go to them—even if that meant going to the highways and byways to find them.

So, I began to knock on doors and run buses. I learned how to get people into church and keep them. Once I learned these important lessons, with God's blessing, I knew they could be applied anywhere in any church. I decided it was time to go to a bigger city where more people needed to be reached for Christ.

However, no one climbs a ladder by starting with the top rung. We have to work our way up from the bottom. Every risk we take prepares us for the greater risk ahead. Rarely does God call us to take an enormous risk when we have never taken any risks before. Instead, He has us begin with the bottom rung, the lowest level of risk on the risk ladder.

From there we are constantly led into stronger, tougher, bolder, higher, riskier decisions for the glory of God. But God will not take us faster than we are able to go. Nor will He allow us to be tempted beyond what we can bear. But line upon line, precept upon precept, He builds us into men and women of faith. That's what the life of faith is all about.

The risk ladder prepared me to face the greater risks I encountered in my ministry in Los Angeles. The rungs on the risk ladder I climbed in Davenport and then Phoenix prepared me for far greater risks and steeper climbs in Los Angeles.

I believe in living the adventure for Jesus, sold out to Him every day. If we do that, our adventures become more and more thrilling.

NINE

The Adventure of Facing Your Fears

He has not learned the lesson of life who does not every day surmount a fear.

—RALPH WALDO EMERSON

ONE OF THE most effective advertisements ever written appeared in a London newspaper in the early 1900s: "Men wanted for hazardous journey. Small wages, bitter cold, long months of complete darkness, constant danger, safe return doubtful."

The ad was written by Sir Ernest Shackleton, explorer of the South Pole. Regarding the ad's response, Shackleton noted, "It seemed as though all the men in Great Britain were determined to accompany us."[1]

We admire those who have no fear. I see people wearing T-shirts and ball caps emblazoned with "No Fear." If only that were true for a greater number of Christians.

FEAR STANDS BETWEEN YOUR ADVENTURE AND YOU

William Seymour was born in Louisiana in 1870 to former slaves. He grew up as a devout Baptist, and as a boy had visions and dreams from God. As a young adult he worked as a waiter and sought God for direction in his life, eventually joining a Holiness church and becoming a preacher. Smallpox robbed him of sight in his left eye, but he pressed on and became pastor of a church in Houston, Texas.

While in Houston in 1905, Seymour heard of a "new" experience called speaking in tongues. Intrigued, he enrolled in a Bible school in Kansas where speaking in tongues was encouraged, but because of the prevailing racial segregation, he was forced to sit in the hall and listen to the lectures through an open doorway. He became convinced that the gift of tongues was for today, although he had not received the gift himself. Upon returning to Houston he was invited to preach at a church in Los Angeles with the possibility of becoming pastor.

His first sermon in Los Angeles was on the subject of speaking in tongues according to Acts 2:4, angering the current pastor who promptly locked him out of the church. Seymour took up residence in a home on Bonnie Brae Street, not far from the present-day Dream Center. There, after several weeks of prayer, he and others were baptized in the Holy Spirit and a local revival began that started to draw crowds by the thousands. As more people came, it was impractical for Seymour to preach from the porch, as was his custom, so they moved to an old building on Azusa Street that had once been a church and was more recently a stable and a warehouse.

The *Los Angeles Times* ran a front page report that talked about the "weird babble of tongues" and "wild scenes" that took place during services, but the article only served to spread the revival. For hours on end, people would praise the Lord, singing hymns and gathering around the altar seeking the baptism of the Holy Spirit.

Seymour would often sit behind the pulpit with his head hidden by a box to avoid being the center of attention while the Holy Spirit moved. He started a periodical called *The Apostolic Faith,* which sent news of this revival to fifty thousand subscribers. People from all over the world made pilgrimages to Azusa Street, and from Azusa went missionaries to every part of the world. For the next several years, Los Angeles was the center of the greatest revival of the twentieth century. That mission on Azusa Street became the fountainhead for the entire Pentecostal and Charismatic Movement of today, which now counts hundreds of millions of adherents all over the world.[2]

But I often wonder, what if Seymour, this half-blind son of former slaves, had given into the fear that surely gripped him when he was invited to speak in Los Angeles? What if he had never felt worthy of being more than a waiter and had missed his calling as a pastor? What if fear instead of faith had written the pages of his life?

When we are going a way we have never been before, and we have no precedent or road map, we may experience fear. Our greatest moments, our Azusa Street, our Promised Land may be right ahead of us, yet fear lies in between. Please understand this: Our enemy is not lack, our enemy is not sickness, our enemy is not a person, place or thing. *The only enemy we have to face is fear.*

Only as we leave familiar surroundings will we experience

dimensions of divine reality never before experienced. The great adventurers in the Bible were men and women who walked by faith. In Hebrews 11 we are told that "by faith Abraham obeyed when he was called to go out to the place which he would receive as an inheritance. And he went out, not knowing where he was going" (v. 8). Many of us would like to walk by faith as Abraham did. But do you know how he became a man of great faith? He left the comforts of his home and set out on a journey not knowing where he was going. Can you hear him? "Mom and Dad, I'm leaving. I don't know where I'm going, when I will be back or how I'll pay my bills. But don't worry. God is in control."

If you lose your job, what is the normal human response? Fear. If someone walks out of your life or a relationship is broken, what is your initial feeling? Fear. Often, when God draws us into new realms of His blessing, our old means of provision will be cut off. So, if your normal provision of income is suddenly cut off, the response of faith says, "Let's just see what new thing the Lord is going to do, because that job was not my source—God is my source."

Coaches often tell their sports teams, "Lose to your opponent, but don't lose to fear." Did you know many teams lose to fear before they even get on the playing field? At the professional level, often the team who believes and has faith beats the team who fears. When we overcome fear, nothing else will be able to defeat us because the root of all defeat is fear.

Some people who die because of cancer don't lose to cancer; they lose to fear. Others think they fail because circumstances are against them. But in reality, they lose to fear.

ADVENTURE YOURSELF

A host of fears plague mankind:

- Fear of public speaking
- Fear of rejection
- Fear of the unknown
- Fear of poverty
- Fear of death
- Fear of embarrassment

Every new idea I have ever tried made me uncomfortable when I first did it. The first time I preached my illustrated sermon "The Whip, the Hammer and the Cross" was at a youth camp in Harrisburg, Pennsylvania. I was a teenage evangelist, and I'll tell you, I was uncomfortable. I worried about whether or not it was too dramatic or too long or too intense. But it was a success in many ways. When I look back, I realize that everything God has used for His glory has made me uneasy at first. I just had to move forward through the fear.

FACING OUR FEARS

Fear isn't to be avoided, but taken head-on. Mark Twain once said, "Courage is resistance to fear, mastery of fear, not absence of fear." In each new stage of life, with each new adventure, we will come face to face with our fears—and our response is most critical.

I have taught my children how to face rather than avoid fearful situations. When Kristie was only twelve, I put her and a friend in charge of a bus route for our bus ministry. I promised to drive the bus, but her responsibility was to work the route—knock on doors, check on kids and invite people to church.

Both Matthew and Luke are good basketball players. When they were still in high school we went on a trip to New York City. I decided to drive them to inner-city Brooklyn to let them play where basketball is really good. We drove around until we found a court where some inner-city youths were playing—kids who really knew how to play. We got out of the car, and I spoke to the youths.

"Where I come from, my sons are pretty good basketball players, but I wanted to take them where people *really* know how to play basketball. Then you can tell me how good they really are." My sons played, and even I got into the game. Those young men said my boys were good, even in the inner city. We need to raise our children not to avoid fear, but to face it and walk through it.

Fear is a faulty member of the decision-making family because it negates God's divine power. God doesn't call us to react in fear but to walk by faith. Faith is the opposite of fear.

People ask me, "Aren't you afraid you're going to get shot when you minister in the inner city?" No, I'm not. When I give in to fear, it controls me. When fear controls me, I make it my god, and God commands us, "You shall have no other gods before Me" (Exod. 20:3).

NEVER FEAR: GOD TAKES CARE OF THE DETAILS

Elijah gave a prophetic word to King Ahab, "There shall not be dew nor rain these years, except at my word" (1 Kings 17:1). God honored Elijah's word, and a drought and a famine prevailed throughout the land. King Ahab held Elijah responsible, so his life was in danger. But the Lord protected Elijah's life by instructing him:

> Get away from here and turn eastward, and hide by
> the Brook Cherith, which flows into the Jordan. And
> it will be that you shall drink from the brook, and I
> have commanded the ravens to feed you there.
>
> —1 KINGS 17:3–4

Elijah heeded God's Word, and his needs were met—even in the midst of lack all around him.

Living the adventure means exposing yourself to risk and danger. If God calls you to a certain place, don't worry about the details. That's where you should be. God sent ravens to feed Elijah while he lived by the brook. Don't move unless God speaks to you personally. But if God calls you, He will feed you.

But what do you do when your provision stops and the brook dries up? Wait for another word from God.

> Then the word of the LORD came to him, saying,
> "Arise, go to Zarephath, which belongs to Sidon,
> and dwell there. See, I have commanded a widow
> there to provide for you."
>
> —1 KINGS 17:8–9

Elijah was once again led by God into a place where he found provision and protection. The point is that you are never, ever left alone when you nurture an intimate relationship with God. Repeatedly in Scripture God promises that He will never ever leave nor forsake the righteous.

We need to spend time in the presence of God so we can recognize when He is leading us ahead. How did God lead Israel through the desert on the way to the Promised Land? He led them by His tangible presence—a cloud by day and fire by night. When they crossed the Jordan River, the Ark of the Covenant–the presence of God–led them. When we leave the comforts of house and home and step out into new realms of faith, we are to be led by the presence of God.

Had I been led by what I could see, I would have never ended up in Phoenix. I was happy in the soft, feathery bed of Davenport, Iowa. After all, I had been invited to open the United States Congress with prayer because our state's senator had just gotten saved in our church. Johnny Cash's two visits helped us set records in Sunday school attendance. People were giving their lives to Christ, and we were one of the fastest-growing churches in the nation. God was moving in a great way–why would I want to leave?

One morning I woke up, and for the first time in my life I felt I had lost the conscious presence of God. I prayed and fasted. I sought the Lord, but still I felt nothing. He was with me, but I just didn't feel His presence.

Often the way God gets our attention is by withdrawing His conscience presence. During that time I prayed, "God, I'll do anything to get Your conscious presence back." That's when a letter landed on my desk that said, "Would you consider coming to pastor in Phoenix, Arizona?" I read it and threw it in the trash. Three days later, the Lord said, "Do what I tell you. Now pick that letter out of the trash and read it again." I read the letter again, and God spoke to my heart to visit Phoenix. When I obeyed God's direction, I once again began feeling His conscious presence.

Moving to Phoenix was a risk. To the intellect, exchanging a congregation of four thousand for a congregation of two hundred didn't make sense. But in my heart it made all the sense in the world.

When Moses sent twelve men to spy out the Promised Land, ten of them reported what their minds concluded about what their eyes saw: obstacles, giants and defeat. But Caleb and Joshua reported what their *hearts* saw: "The giants are big, but our God is bigger!" (See Numbers 13–14.) When facing insurmountable odds, good "heart sight" is more important than good eyesight.

We have to go with what our hearts see.

When people warn, "The sky is falling," we have to decide whose report we are going to believe—theirs or God's. Are we going to believe the enemy is too big and head back to Egypt? Or are we going to believe what God says—that we can take the land? "If God is for us, who can be against us?" (Rom. 8:31). We can believe God when He says, "You are going a way that you have never gone before, but I'll go with you." We have to take the leap of faith just as Caleb and Joshua did. Then we will reap the rewards of faith just as they did.

FAITH IS FOSTERED IN GOD'S PRESENCE

Faith is not an option for the Christian. "But without faith it is impossible to please Him, for he who comes to God must believe that He is, and that He is a rewarder of those who diligently seek Him" (Heb. 11:6). When we respond in fear rather than faith, it is impossible to please God and walk in His blessing. To move forward into the adventure we must believe not only that He exists, but that He also rewards those who "diligently seek Him." That means God rewards people who actively seek the conscious presence of Jesus Christ.

Faith isn't something we conjure up ourselves. The

apostle Paul wrote, "So then faith comes by hearing, and hearing by the word of God" (Rom. 10:17). We need faith to please God, but the Bible also tells us faith only comes from God. So how are we supposed to walk in something we cannot generate for ourselves? We must spend time in God's presence so His faith will rub off on us. We must be led by our heart more than our head and remain sensitive to where His presence is leading us.

John Wesley once said:

> Give me a hundred men who fear nothing but sin, and desire nothing but God and I will shake the world. I care not a straw whether they be clergymen or laymen; and such alone will overthrow the kingdom of Satan and build up the kingdom of God on earth.

The presence of God is the breeding ground of faith and courage. Fearlessly attempting to do something great for God apart from His guidance is merely foolhardiness. But when we get into the presence of God and let God's presence lead us, we will break through fear into the great adventure of faith.

TEN

The Adventure of Reaching Every Creature

God's work done in God's way will never lack God's supplies.

—J. HUDSON TAYLOR

OUR THREE-YEAR search for a new facility had formally come to an end—and not a moment too soon. We had housed new converts in the unoccupied houses included with our Bethel Temple property. With about two hundred people living in the residences, we were filled to capacity. However, the "no vacancy" sign was heavy on my heart because it shut out hundreds waiting to be discipled.

THE HOME FOR THE DREAM

Several years before when George Wood and I were

driving on the Hollywood Freeway, I noticed a huge, impressive building that dwarfed the hill upon which it stood. The Queen of Angels hospital could be seen from every direction. Fifteen stories high, it was located between Los Angeles and Hollywood in one of the roughest neighborhoods in the nation.

The Queen of Angels nine-acre property held the hospital plus eight other buildings. The hospital itself boasted fourteen hundred rooms—many with private baths—for a capacity of three thousand guests. All the buildings on the campus contained a total of 400,000 square feet. This facility could house a small town!

Four years previous, the facility had been listed for sale at a price of $16 million. The estimated replacement value: $50 million. Now the property was on the market for the greatly reduced price of $6 million.

Standing on the grounds of this historic hospital gave me new enthusiasm and hope for the work God was doing in Los Angeles. I began praising and thanking God in advance for the new births that would emerge from this complex. Ideas for reaching the poor and destitute of the city raced through my mind.

The prayer chapel would occupy the top floor of the hospital. Another floor would serve as an AIDS hospice, since our new facility was divinely positioned right in the midst of a large homosexual community.

Often after a gang member is seriously injured from a gunshot, he is discarded like trash and has no place to go. One floor would be dedicated to caring for the hundreds of gang members who were crippled as a result of these senseless gang wars. Our wheelchair-accessible buses could provide the transportation to fill the front of our meeting places with these young men.

One floor would be dedicated to unwed mothers. I thought about my conversations with Nancy Alcorn and her great work with pregnant young girls. Possibly she would come and help us. Perhaps another floor would be reserved for different ethnic worship services. We could serve food to the homeless in the cafeteria, with plenty of space left over for a clothing room.

I also saw the need for dedicating a floor solely for pastors and Christian workers who were discouraged and burned out. This former hospital could be a place for spiritual renewal, restoration and recovery.

We knew this was the place for the ministry, so we began negotiations, eventually settling on the price of $3.9 million. With deep emotions and solemn gratitude to God in our hearts we signed the escrow papers. It was not the end of the journey—it was a new beginning.

THE COST OF THE DREAM

Our sales contract had this stipulation: We had to come up with $500,000 within thirty days, and we had eighteen months to pay off the remaining $3.4 million.

Over the next month I went on the road sharing with other churches the vision Matthew and I had for the Dream Center. Offerings came in at a surprising pace: $20,000, $30,000, $50,000 at a time. Within a month we had raised $500,000!

And the miracles continued. A businessman from my church gave $1 million, and his son followed suit with another million. All totaled, our donations amounted to $2.5 million. We sold the Bethel Temple building for $1.4

million, bringing us to our required $3.9 million sale price.

But we discovered that paying off the property was just the first step. The buildings required retrofitting. The wiring had to be brought up to code, along with myriad other upgrades. It was a costly proposition, but not expensive when compared to the value of souls.

Even after the property was paid off, the donations kept pouring in. Gifts of $1,000, $5,000, even $10,000 came in to help refurbish the building. People were catching the vision for reaching the lost and hurting in the inner city.

Despite the repairs that were required, the city of Los Angeles issued us a temporary occupancy permit, allowing us to inhabit the building until it was brought up to code. We took occupancy in July 1995 when the first three hundred people became initial residents of one of the hospital's annex buildings and two of the former nurses' residences. Our deadline for getting the building up to code was February 1998.

SHARING THE DREAM OF COMPASSION

The Queen of Angels hospital was named for Mary, the mother of Jesus. Wanting our spiritual hospital to be a place where dreams are not only given birth, but also come true, we christened the former hospital "the Dream Center."

The dream for the Queen of Angels hospital was born in 1925 in the heart of a Franciscan sister of the Sacred Heart. After the Franciscan sisters voluntarily left Germany in the late nineteenth century, they established hospitals down the California coast beginning in San Francisco in 1904, Santa Barbara in 1916 and Los Angeles in 1926. Noble and well-educated, the women possessed a wonderful command of various European languages, which benefited them as they reached into the community.

The unique location of the Queen of Angels positioned them to minister to the burgeoning Los Angeles population during its rapid growth throughout the twentieth century. Consistently through the years the Franciscan sisters modeled love and compassion. People were given quality medical care irrespective of their ability to pay.

Their work was not established without sacrifice and struggle. In a compiled history of the first forty years, Dr. Robert Blackmum wrote:

> How could a hospital such as Queen of Angels, so strategically located to the medical fraternity, so fine in spirit, so fully dedicated to patient care, so central to the economic heart of a metropolis, so free-swinging in service, so unlimited in capability, remain so bereft of large-scale financial support?

In reading those words I felt a new dedication to our work. My hope was that our people would be as committed to laboring compassionately as those who had gone before us had been. Yet I secretly hoped we would not be so bereft of large-scale financial support.

Those were some of the scariest moments of my life, but we encountered the Holy Spirit's miracle-working power time and again. And I never felt closer to God.

I hear people pray, "O God, I want the same kind of faith Daniel had." But I wonder, *Do you—really?* The Daniel kind of faith is forged in the lion's den. For instance, every day is still a walk of faith as our needs require $350,000 per month just to operate this giant soul-winning machine. To bring the building up to required city standards that will allow us to house 2,500 people would require another $3 million.

Other people pray, "O God, I want miracles in my life." So God responds, "Good, I've been waiting for you to say that. I'm going to place you in a situation where you get so desperate for a miracle that we can work one together." That's the excitement of the breathtaking adventure of the Holy Spirit in our lives.

TO EVERY CREATURE

I believe a special anointing comes when we are involved in kingdom work. Jesus' last command before ascending into heaven was this: "Go ye into all the world, and preach the gospel to every creature" (Mark 16:15, kjv). Let's look at the word *creature*.

We have "creatures" in this world today—teenagers with purple hair, forty earrings in each earlobe, three in each nostril, two in each lip, one hanging from each cheekbone and a spiked leather collar full around their necks. The tendency among most people—Christians as well—is to avoid creatures who look, act or live different from us. Yet Jesus calls us to take the gospel to every *creature*.

Obeying Jesus' command goes against our self-preservation instincts. It will be time-consuming, expensive and dangerous. It may cost us our lives or the lives of our children.

Our natural impulse then is, having found Jesus Christ, to gather with other people who have found Jesus Christ and form a secret little club—a Christian "gang," if you please. We develop hand signals, rituals and Christian jargon that outsiders don't understand. This succeeds in keeping them on the outside. In this gang, a fortress mentality develops, shielding Christians from creatures unlike themselves. The church becomes a fortress instead of a hospital. This fortress does not protect us against Satan and his forces, but keeps out the very people for whom Jesus died.

DO WE BUILD FORTRESSES OR INVITE IN CREATURES?

A modern phenomenon in the Phoenix area of late is the emergence of gated and walled communities. In order to protect ourselves from crime, we have built walled cities—suburban fortresses, if you will.

Protecting ourselves and our assets from danger is understandable. But we in churches tend to build invisible walls that keep us from the different kinds of creatures on the outside. That collides with the mandate of Jesus Christ to "go ye into all the world and preach the gospel to every creature."

Many of the churches in Los Angeles have fences built around them for protection. They keep out the very people God has called them to reach. At the Dream Center, we have no fences. God has called us not to build fences but to tear them down.

Initially I had visions that the wealthy of Los Angeles, after experiencing our dream for the inner city, would flock to the Dream Center to help pay the bills. We invited numerous people to be our guests, but letters arrived in the mail saying, "We would like to come, but we're concerned for our safety. We're afraid that after dark our cars will get ripped off."

The parable Jesus told in Luke 14 came to mind. When

the respectable were invited to a banquet, each one had an excuse for not coming. Reluctant to squander his generosity, the master then commanded his servants to go out and get the poor, the crippled, the blind and the lame—to get the dregs of the city and *compel them to come in* so he could have a full house (Luke 14:23). We're not supposed to leave the poor and destitute to fend for themselves. We're supposed to get our hands dirty and bring them in to our sterilized churches with our clean carpeting and brand-spanking-new pews. There is no person so derelict that he or she is beyond the love of Jesus. Every church should have a well-used welcome mat at its sanctuary door.

We take the call to carry the gospel to every creature very seriously. When we moved into the Queen of Angels hospital, we mounted a neon sign in the lobby that reads, "Welcome sinners." All people—believers or non-believers—are created with an addiction to sin, a sinful nature. Until nonbelievers can readily acknowledge they're sinners, the blood of Jesus will be powerless to wash away their sins. Additionally, until believers can readily acknowledge they're sinners also, they will be ineffective in reaching the lost. That sign is a reminder that we all stand on level ground at the foot of the cross.

REACHING CREATURES OF ALL SHAPES AND SIZES

At the Dream Center, we invited ministries that had previously been unconnected to come under our ministry umbrella. Within two years, one hundred fifty smaller ministries made up the Los Angeles International Church. Some groups using the facility came under our direct oversight, but other independent groups use our facility in what we call "a common struggle to help the afflicted and spread God's Word."

We require all five hundred of our church staff members and volunteers to donate five hours a week to serving poor neighborhoods, doing everything from distributing food to washing cars to painting apartment buildings.

Part of the service we give comes in the form of our Adopt-a-Block program. Since moving into the Dream Center, every Saturday from 10 A.M. to 2 P.M. the entire staff breaks into different groups and goes into the surrounding neighborhoods to pick up trash and invite families to church.

At first, the response from the community was suspicious and hostile. Wary gang members let us know we weren't welcome on their turf. But through acts of kindness, we befriended them. As people's lives were touched, our church grew. As our church grew, more blocks were added. As more blocks were added, more people came on Sunday, and our church grew even more. Within two years we were cleaning up forty-five blocks.

We began reaching drug addicts, alcoholics, prostitutes, gang members, battered women, unwed mothers, abused children, runaways and homeless people. We developed a job training center and a program to tutor young students after school. We started a ministry to the children in our community called Metro Kidz, which presents the gospel in over twenty-seven locations every week, reaching seven thousand children.

We acquired sixteen buses (including four wheelchair buses) and six vans to transport people from the surrounding community and two Mack trucks to haul in donated food. Our soup kitchen is open every day, serving fifteen hundred hot meals a day for those who live at the Dream Center, plus providing food for twenty thousand more families. We also started producing the Dream Center television program on the Trinity Broadcasting Network and eleven other stations.

Reaching out to the various ethnic groups in the area was an important priority for us. Now we hold church services in eleven different languages. A discipleship program was established to gird up the vast number of people who were dedicating their lives to Christ. My son Matthew says, "If they're not changed inside, they're going to go back on the street."

At one of our first church services, people came in from the gangs, the projects and the bars. Some were dressed in leather, and others were wearing suits. We looked like the United Nations, with Caucasians, Hispanics, Asians and African Americans all in attendance. The occupants of the front row looked as if they had been lifted from the bar scene in *Star Wars*. It was the rowdiest service I had ever seen. Yet at the altar call, at least one hundred or more responded to the invitation to give their lives to Jesus.

After they all prayed, I said, "Stand up now and give a cheer to the Lord." Everybody gave a cheer to the Lord, and then I said, "Now, let's give it to the devil tonight. I'm going to count to three, and I want you to either shake your fist or yell out something to the devil. Just give the devil a fit."

When they told the devil what a dirty guy he was, Matthew later told me, "Dad, one of those guys who just got saved made an obscene hand gesture to the devil!" Now, I'm not advocating this kind of behavior, but it's indicative of the world in which we live.

These people need to be taught character and protocol.

The homosexual community frightens us. Gang members frighten us. The violence that we see in L.A. frightens us. On one of our buses, a teenage gang member told one of our young Master's Commission girls that he would blow her head off. Two young people have been killed on the block right in front of the church. But we have to move beyond our fears to take the gospel to every creature.

Matthew won the confidence of local gang members and had them promise that if he brought members of other gangs to the Dream Center, they would leave them alone. They told Matthew they loved him and that the church was neutral ground. What a victory!

If we will venture away from the safety of our comfort zones and share the life-giving Good News of Jesus Christ with every creature, we will see lives changed. We'll see miracles taking place in our lives. Then we'll be so hooked on the adventure that we'll never want to go back.

I preached in a church in Nebraska recently. After the service was over, a beautiful young lady came up to me and said, "I used to be in your church. You wouldn't recognize me from what I used to look like. I was nothing but an alcoholic and a drug-dealing prostitute, but I rode your buses. Your church was the only church in America that would have accepted me. Now I'm married, my life is back together again and most of all, I belong to Jesus."

I gave her a big hug, and then she introduced me to her husband. What if someone had said, "We don't want that dirty little prostitute in our church—she might infect our kids"? Where would she be today?

Taking the gospel to every creature will get your hands dirty, but the dividends are out of this world!

ELEVEN

The Adventure of Faithfulness

Faith is dead to doubt, dumb to discouragement, blind to impossibilities and knows nothing but success in God.

—Anonymous

I F I WERE to ask you to list some people who had great adventures, whom would you name? Perhaps Lewis and Clark, the American explorers of the Northwest, or Neil Armstrong, the first man to set foot on the moon. Maybe you'd pick Admiral Richard Byrd, the man who led five expeditions to Antarctica and who was the first man to fly over the North Pole. Or maybe Clara Barton, known for her brave medical care on battlefields both in the United States and in Europe and for founding the American Red Cross. Many missionaries would also deserve our praise.

But allow me to share with you an adventure I observed in our church parking lot in Phoenix not long ago. Every week a certain man brings his wife to church in a wheel-chair. He passes through the same door every Sunday morning, shakes my hand and talks to me, always including his wife in the conversation. One Sunday following our worship service, I was shaking hands with the last few people when I noticed this couple leaving. Fascinated, I followed behind from close range and listened in on their "adventure of faithfulness."

"Oh, honey, there is Sister So and So over there—remember her? Remember what she gave you for your birthday? Isn't she a lovely lady?"

His wife stared glassily ahead. I don't know the nature of her infirmity—maybe she has Alzheimer's, or perhaps a stroke has affected her ability to respond.

Lovingly, the husband continued, "Oh, sweetheart, look at that car. Remember, we had a car years ago that looked a lot like that one." He walked a little further and remarked, "Oh, look at Sister So and So's dress!" His wife never moved. It seemed as if she hadn't heard a thing.

He stopped for a moment, walked around to the front of her wheelchair, talked to her some more, then pulled out a handkerchief and carefully wiped the saliva that had run down the side of her mouth. Then he bent over and gently kissed her on the cheek.

THE LONG-TERM ADVENTURE

This man is on an adventure vastly more difficult than climbing Mt. Everest, or even stepping on the moon. He is on an adventure of faithfulness, one of God's highest and most unrecognized callings.

Faithfulness is long-term responsibility, and it can last a

lifetime. Few people stand on the sidelines and applaud those who are on the adventure of faithfulness. You see, faithfulness is inglorious. The adventure is not based on thrills or excitement but on devotion and fidelity. Nonetheless, this adventure does probe deep into the unknown—the unknown of pain and patience.

The husband I watched that day could have said to himself, *This isn't fair. Why should I have to be saddled with this lady? There are places I want to go, people I'd like to meet. My life is on hold while I care for a person who has no possibility of ever returning my love. I am missing out on adventures because I have to take care of her.* But instead, he chose to take the adventure of faithfulness because he recognizes its importance.

HOPE DEFERRED AND THE AGONY OF THE SOUL

Usually, we think of faith as being stirring, challenging, thrilling and exciting. And at times it is. But often overlooked in the life of faith is the agony of the soul. In Hebrews we read about the nature of faith: "Now faith is the substance of things hoped for, the evidence of things not seen" (Heb. 11:1). Notice that it says, "hoped for." Hope indicates an expectation of something good in the future. In other words, hope looks forward to something it doesn't yet have. Therein lies the agony.

A verse in Proverbs sheds more light on the agony of faith: "Hope deferred makes the heart sick, but when the desire comes, it is a tree of life" (13:12). Faith is the substance of things hoped for, but the longer our hope is delayed, the sicker our waiting hearts grow and the greater the agony. And we wonder, *How long can I hold on? How much longer must I wait for this deferred hope to come to pass?*

Years ago I read a biography of Andrew Murray, the eminent pastor who led South Africa into a great time of revival during the latter half of the nineteenth century. Although he is known for his leadership in the South African revival, he had little to do with its beginning. Prior to his arrival in Worcester, South Africa, Murray's father, John, prayed unwaveringly for years that God would send revival to his church. But seemingly, his prayers went unanswered. Andrew then joined his father in the pulpit, and together they prayed another seven years. Over thirty years of prayer ascended to God for revival in South Africa until they began to despair they would ever see it at all.

One Sunday during the evening service, sixty young people in an adjoining room began making such a loud commotion that it disrupted the adult meeting. Following the adult service, an elder looked in on the young people's meeting to discover what was causing the disturbance. After seeing the youth on their knees wailing in prayer, he called for Andrew Murray. Murray walked into the room and yelled, "People, silence!" But the young people continued wailing and praying. Agitated, Murray yelled again, "People, I am your minister, sent from God. *Silence!*" Once again, the noise continued.

Stomping out of the hall, Murray gathered the adults and led them in a rousing rendition of the Dutch hymn, "Aid the Soul That Helpless Cries." Obviously, he was unable to recognize that God had answered his prayers.

One last time, Andrew Murray entered the hall where the young people were praying and announced, "God is a God of order, and here everything is confusion." With that he walked out.

Revival meetings were held every evening after that. Within the week, Murray recognized the hand of God and began leading his congregation—and South Africa—into revival.

For over thirty years Andrew Murray's father contended faithfully in prayer. Certainly John Murray's heart was sick in agony as he awaited an outpouring of the Holy Spirit. How many people do you think would have waited even one year, much less twenty, ten or five?[1]

I believe if a person is able to hold onto a dream for five years, it will come to pass. But few people are willing to persevere that long. Instead they get discouraged. The doubt peddler comes, and the agony of hope deferred causes them to lose heart. I wonder how many adventures would have been taken had people not turned back? What revivals were forfeited by default? How many people would have been saved? What miracles would God have worked?

GOD'S ALL-SUFFICIENT GRACE

There have been moments in my life when I couldn't continue in my own strength—times when I was reduced to absolute weakness. I just wanted to give up. That's when I grasped the hem of the Master's garment and said, "I have nothing. I can't do this. I can't face this."

Jesus' great promise to us is found in Paul's letter to the Corinthians: "My grace is sufficient for you, for My strength is made perfect in weakness" (2 Cor. 12:9). In the inglorious adventure of faithfulness, I find my strength comes from God. Only in those moments of weakness—when I can no longer rely on my own wisdom, strength and abilities, when I lack the wherewithal to make it even through the morning—do I prove that He is strong.

On a business trip to London, a wealthy Texan decided he wanted to purchase a Rolls Royce. After looking around the showroom and test-driving the car, he remarked to the salesman who was assisting him, "I like your cars, and I know which one I want. But before I buy it, would you tell me how much horsepower this Rolls Royce has?"

"It is the policy of the Rolls Royce Corporation never to divulge how much horsepower the engine has," the salesman politely answered.

"Well, I may be in London, but I am a Texan, and I am concerned about horsepower. I am not going to buy this Rolls until I know how much horsepower it has."

The salesman turned around, walked into his office, shut the door and called his manager on the phone. "I have a man ready to buy. He's prepared to pay cash, but he refuses to buy the car unless he knows the horsepower of the Rolls. What should I say?"

The voice at the other end of the line answered, "We will not tell him."

The salesman pleaded with his manager, "*Please*, give me some kind of an answer."

"Tell him that the horsepower is sufficient," the manager calmly responded.

God answers us with those same words. In our agony we cry out to Him, "How much grace do You have? I don't know how much more of this agony I can take!"

And He calmly answers, "My grace is sufficient."

FAITH AND FAITHFULNESS

We think of someone who is *faithful* as being earnest,

steadfast, trustworthy and dependable, as the elderly man was with his wife in the wheelchair.

But there's another perspective on the meaning of being faithful:

> Paul, an apostle of Jesus Christ by the will of God, to the saints who are in Ephesus, and *faithful* in Christ Jesus.
>
> —EPHESIANS 1:1, EMPHASIS ADDED

Paul refers to people who have placed their faith in Christ Jesus as the "faithful."

It may seem obvious, but there is a direct connection between having faith and being faithful. To be full of faith means to be faith*ful*. When we are faithful, our internal faith is shown by our outward actions.

Why would a man rob a liquor store? Because he does not believe God will provide what he needs. Why would a woman kill her husband? Because she doesn't believe that either God can provide her with the grace to live with the bum or change him somewhere down the line. So she takes the law into her own hands and kills him.

Why would a woman abort a precious baby? Because she lacks the faith to believe God will provide enough money to pay her bills as she goes through the adventure of faith. She may question whether God can provide the strength to endure the scandal of an illegitimate pregnancy. Perhaps she cannot deal with the possibility that the child could be born afflicted or deformed. Because she is not full of faith, she is unable to be faithful.

Why do we state in our marriage vows, "For better or worse, for richer or poorer, in sickness and in health, till death do us part"? Because with our vows we are saying, "You can count on me to be faithful because I believe that God's grace is sufficient. I am counting on God, so you can count on me."

Faithfulness, then, is rooted in faith. As we believe in God's ability to meet us at the point of our need, we will be faithful. You see, many adventures will shape our futures, but faithfulness actually shapes *us*. Our faithfulness is the measuring stick of our faith.

Years ago when I was a young evangelist, I preached on a Sunday morning when Elvis Presley was in the audience. He grew up attending an Assemblies of God church and continued to do so off and on throughout his career. Following the morning service he met privately with the senior pastor. He was weeping because God had spoken to his heart, and as he sat there with his girlfriend, the pastor told him, "Elvis, you know you need to get your life right with Jesus Christ."

"But I have contracts that bind me for the next twenty years," he replied. "And what if I renounce show business and find that serving God won't bring joy to my heart?"

In other words, Elvis was saying, "I don't believe that God's grace is sufficient." Unfortunately, show business never did bring joy to Elvis's heart, and he died of heart failure hastened by constant barbiturate use.

I could march in front of you an army of young men and women once hopelessly bound by drugs and alcohol. But God proved that His grace was greater than their sins. I could show you couples who wouldn't be married today except for God's all-sufficient grace.

Our ability to be faithful rests upon our level of faith in the power of God. Without faith, we won't be faithful.

STAY FAITHFUL AND DON'T GIVE UP

There once were several successful businessmen who were practical jokers. As a matter of fact, these men organized an informal club just for jokers. All the members worked in a glass skyscraper in a major U.S. city, and during the noon hour, they would play practical jokes on people passing by.

One of their favorite pranks involved a stone building across the street, which they could see from their office windows. Away from plain sight a nail had been affixed to the side of the building. During the noon hour, one of the pranksters would wrap a string around the nail and then pull it around the corner of the building.

Wearing a hard hat and yellow road construction clothes, the prankster would stretch the string out as though he were making measurements. Alternately looking at the string and then the street, he would stop a passerby and ask, "Would you hold this string for a minute? I have to run an errand, and I'll be right back. But it's *very* important that you hold this string."

Oftentimes the innocent bystander would agree to hold the string while the man ran across the street and into the building. There, the club members would observe from their offices and laugh at their victim. Very few of the passersby would stay very long. As soon as the man was out of sight, most of them would just drop the string and leave. But some of them would wait a little longer. Eventually, when they realized they had been played for the fool, they would drop the string and leave.

One day, a man was riding down the street on his bike. He had a cowboy hat on and a little red flag on the back that stood up straight like an arrow. He was slow, perhaps with Down's syndrome. One of the pranksters stopped him and asked, "Hey, buddy. Wait just a minute, I need some help. Will you help me?"

"Sure I will," he answered as he dismounted his bike. The man then began his pitch, "Would you hold this string for me until I get back? This is *very* important."

"Yes," came the reply.

Quickly the man handed the string over. He then scampered across the street into his office building where he took off his hard hat and laughed along with his partners in crime.

When these smug, arrogant businessmen went up to their glass tower and looked down, they saw the young man standing patiently, holding the string. The noon hour passed, but he continued holding on to that string.

Two o'clock, he was still honoring the man's request.

Three o'clock came, and he could be seen diligently holding on to the string despite the increasingly hot and humid July weather.

Around four o'clock, the thick humidity deteriorated into a torrential downpour. Yet the man stood there, immovable. His cowboy hat drooped around his ears, but he stood, wet to the bone.

Buckling under his increasing guilt, the prankster rushed down to the young man, thanked him and brought him upstairs. There the men cleaned him up, offered to pay him for his time and apologized. "We are so sorry for what we did to you. Would you ever forgive us?"

Despite their repeated explanations, the young man couldn't understand that a joke had been played on him. He was just proud that he had waited until they came back.

That precious man with Down's syndrome wasn't gifted

or talented. But he proved that diligence requires character more than competence. The man waited patiently without any expectation of reward. How much more do we have something to look forward to who belong to Jesus Christ!

If you are facing a situation that is tempting you to give up, my encouragement to you is this: Hold on. Be faithful, and don't let go of the string. God's grace is sufficient to carry you through just as He has in the past. You may not understand why you're stuck in the middle of storm, but if you hold on, you *will* receive the reward of the agony of an adventure delayed.

> Let us not become weary in doing good, for at the proper time we will reap a harvest if we do not give up.
>
> —GALATIANS 6:9, NIV

TWELVE

The Adventure of Others

David Livingstone's body is here, but his heart is in Africa.

—WRITTEN ON LIVINGSTONE'S GRAVE MARKER

HE WAS BOTH an up-and-coming medical doctor and an educated theologian from Scotland. Sensing a call to take the gospel of Jesus Christ to Africa, in 1840 he boarded a boat in Great Britain and sailed to Africa. Boldy pressing into regions previously unexplored by any white man, he charted his travels for future explorers. To this day, he ranks as one of the great explorers of the African continent. But as effective as he was as an explorer, he was even more effective as a medical missionary.

Twenty-five years later, an American writer asked the question: "Whatever happened to this explorer of great renown?" Nobody knew.

After a fruitless international inquiry, the man behind the search decided to find this person for himself. A news correspondent for the *New York Herald,* H. M. Stanley's search took him throughout central Africa seeking this legendary hero. But his searches were to no avail. In the process, however, he himself became an explorer as his travels brought him down rivers into new, unexplored territory that he mapped out as well. He almost gave up, but a year after his search had begun, Stanley heard there was an old man with white hair in the heart of the Belgian Congo helping dying natives infected with fever.

Upon reaching the man he so desperately sought, Stanley is now immortalized by his famous words: "Dr. Livingstone, I presume."

Together, Stanley and Livingstone explored previously uncharted regions north of Lake Tanganyika in present-day Burundi. As their travels together concluded, Stanley asked him, "You've done a great work. You're a legend in Great Britain, but now you're old. Why don't you come back with me? You'll be a hero, and you can die with the people you love back home."

"Let me pray about it," Livingstone responded. The next day he confessed to Stanley, "I can't return. I'm infected with the same fever that I am treating, and besides, these are the people I love right here."

Respecting Livingstone's request, H. M. Stanley left his newfound friend and returned to New York.

After Stanley departed, Dr. Livingstone prayed, "Dear God, I'm old in body and spirit, dying with disease. Please take me before another year has passed."

A year later Dr. Livingstone died while on his knees in prayer.

Upon hearing word of his death, Great Britain sent a search party to bring Livingstone's body back for a burial befitting a man of his stature. When the party arrived to retrieve the body, the natives refused. "Livingstone's body belongs to us," they insisted. Tensions arose between one of the great powers of the world and this small tribe of indigenous people.

When the peopled realized they were overmatched, one of their men took a dagger, ripped open Livingstone's chest and removed the heart of this great adventurer. As they gave the dead body to their antagonists, they said, "You can take his body, but you can't take his heart. David Livingstone's heart belongs to us."

David Livingstone was given a proper British burial befitting a hero. This great adventurer's body is ensconced in Westminster Abbey amidst many of the greatest people in world history—a medical missionary buried beside kings, queens and elder statesmen. I've been to Westminster Abbey and visited his grave. By his grave lies a sign that reads: "David Livingstone's body is here, but his heart is in Africa." The heart of a true adventurer.

David Livingstone had a brother named John. One day the two brothers were discussing their life goals after Sunday school. John shared with David, "When I grow up, I want to be rich and famous." David replied, "My goal is to follow Christ to the fullest." John eventually reached his goal, and his name is listed in an old edition of the *Encyclopaedia Britannica*. David Livingstone became a renowned medical missionary and explorer of Africa. But how is John remembered? On his tombstone the epitaph reads: "Here lies the brother of David Livingstone."[1]

David Livingstone learned the adventure of others. John Livingstone didn't.

JESUS' ADVENTURE OF OTHERS

Jesus didn't see others as problems or impositions. He regarded them as adventures waiting to happen. I love the words captured in Mark 10:45 when Jesus said, "For even the Son of Man did not come to be served, but to serve, and to give his life as a ransom for many" (NIV).

Jesus accepted others as they were. How I wish I was more like Him in that way! A young man once walked into the Dream Center who utterly horrified me. His long hair, eyelids and eyebrows were all colored coal-black. His face, on the other hand, was painted pale white with black markings on each side of his eyes. Adding insult to injury, He had a dentist remove four of his top front teeth, leaving him with a gaping hole and just his eye-teeth on either side. He looked like a vampire. I asked him what his name was, and he answered, "Damion."

Over and over, Damion would respond to the altar call Matthew or I would give, and then he would leave. One day, he walked up to me and said, "I want to talk to you, preacher."

"OK." I was ready to find out who he was.

"People wonder why I look the way that I do. The only reason I dress like this is to draw attention to myself. I don't want to be another statistic in this city, someone nobody knows is here. I'm kinda famous around here because of the way I dress. People know who Damion is. But I have problems, too. Look at my wrists." As he held his arms up in the air, I could see his wrists were scored up and down with scars from multiple cuts.

"I've been in big trouble, preacher," he continued. "But when I come here, I just feel so good. It's the only time I am happy. When I go back to my old friends, I'm unhappy."

"Damion," I challenged him, "you need to separate yourself from your old friends and your unhappy life and get away. What you need to do is change the way you look and move into the Dream Center." He followed my advice and moved into one of our houses off campus. He is now one of the best workers we have at the Dream Center. Although his appearance has changed, the greatest change has been in Damion's heart.

Since his arrival, a few people have said to me, "If Damion is there, I know the devil must have a foothold at the Dream Center." Some lack the tolerance to give him room to grow. But God is doing a great work in his life. We so quickly forget Paul's words: "But God demonstrates I Iis own love toward us, in that *while we were still sinners,* Christ died for us" (Rom. 5:8, emphasis added).

In Jesus' day, the townspeople in the country of the Gadarenes knew demonized men were living in the tombs, but we see no evidence they ever tried to minister to them. (See Mark 5.) As a matter of fact, they seemed to want the men to remain as they were. That same religious spirit is often alive in the church. "Let them remain lost. This is about us, this is about me, this is about my house, my family and no one else. Our highest priority is to keep the church a safe place." Now people may not say those words, but their actions reveal their hearts.

If we are going to take the adventure of others, we must accept people as they are.

Jesus knew the joy of ministry.

I believe the joy in so many Christians' lives has been stymied because they are not involved in true ministry. The only difference between the Dead Sea and the Red Sea is that the Red Sea has an outflow. Because the Dead Sea never flows out into other bodies of water, it remains dead. In the same way, Christians who do not have a valid outlet in ministry become deader and deader and deader.

Not only are these people dead, but like the townspeople in the Gadarenes, they want everybody else to remain dead, too. I'm amazed at the number of Christians who do not want to reach hurting people. They don't want to run buses. They have a problem with everybody and everything. All they do is gather in their little churches and criticize other churches for playing "the numbers game" or for "compromising the gospel."

Unless your motive is souls, you are not going to run buses, nor will you buy a hospital that requires every last penny of money and every last ounce of energy just to keep it operating. You won't feed people and clothe them free of charge, and you won't hold a pageant that requires you to come every night when your body so desperately cries out for rest—not unless you are there to win souls.

When people see how God can use them to make a difference in *their* world and for the kingdom of God, they learn the joy of ministry. Unfortunately, some Christians live their entire lives never experiencing the joy of praying with someone to accept Christ. Some have never witnessed the power of the gospel at work. The townspeople who ran Jesus off should have said, "Jesus, why don't You stay awhile, heal our sick and show us the way to God? And why don't You teach us how to make a difference in people's lives the way You did to those two demoniacs?" But instead, they said, "Get out. We don't want You here."

If we are going to take the adventure of others, we must know the joy of ministry.

Jesus took delight in showing people who they could be in Christ.

Just as Jesus knew who He was, He delighted in showing other people who they were in His light. That's what the adventure of others is—seeing people become fulfilled in Jesus Christ. It's like searching for gold or diamonds in your house, then suddenly realizing that the diamonds you are searching for are people.

A few years ago, a young man named John came from the L.A. church and shared his story with our people in Phoenix. At a young age John began to commit crimes that would earn him respect in the gang, crimes that would change his life forever. By the time he was older, he had earned a position for himself in his gang in Los Angeles.

John and his family were at a fellow gang member's house for dinner one night when there was a knock at the door. His friend answered the door, only to be confronted by a rival gang member who opened fire into the home. John escaped the gunfire, but not before his wife, two children and a friend were killed. While dodging bullets, he was able to recognize the man firing the gun.

John's sole quest became stalking the killer and avenging the deaths of his wife and children. Eventually he learned about a party the killer would be attending. With Uzis in hand, John and his friends went to the party, opened the door and mowed down many people while they were dancing—including his family's killer.

Later John and his friends were arrested and went to trial. Because the jury saw John was acting out of revenge for his family's tragic death, he was given a minimal sentence and released on parole.

When John came to the Dream Center he was a lonely, bitter man. But Jesus reached into this fellow's heart and transformed his life. Today he is one of our greatest evangelists. Looking at him now, you would never know he was once a murderer. But because he belongs to Jesus, John is no longer a murderer. This gentle man's heart is so broken and remorseful for what he did in the past that he says he is going to win as many souls as he can.

Recently he attended a friend's wedding in Dallas. While walking down the street there, he heard a voice cry out, "John!" His first thought was, *Oh, no! An old enemy has caught up with me.* He spun around and saw a friend from the old gang in L.A.

This large man, plastered with tattoos everywhere, probably could have broken John in half. "John, I've come to Dallas to set up the 18th Street gang, and I want to take you with me so you can meet the gang members."

John replied, "You need to know that I am different now. There have been some big changes in my life."

"I don't care," he said. "Come on."

They took John's car, and while John drove, his friend took out four pounds of cocaine and said, "Come on, have a snort."

"I told you, I've made some big changes," John answered back. "Let me tell you what has happened in my life." He then explained how he came to know Jesus. As John began sharing, his friend screamed at him to stop. John pulled off to the side of the road, calmed his friend down a little, pulled back onto the road and then continued where he left off.

Finally, the man began to cry, "Nothing is going right for me. I'm sick of this way of life. Help me." So John led him to Jesus Christ! When they finished, the man said, "I'm going to meet with the gang right now, and you need to tell them what Jesus has done for you."

Sixty gang members were present, and John was scared to death. The gang members thought John was bringing news of a new shipment of drugs or money to be made, but instead, he shared the good news of what Jesus had done.

While John was speaking, a man threw his bag of drugs down at his side and another man threw down a syringe. John later told me, "Pastor Barnett, I've seen you give altar calls, so I decided to do it the way you do it. I said, 'While every head is bowed and every eye is closed, when I count to three, raise your hand.' I was so scared that I kept my eyes closed until I got to 'three.' When I opened my eyes, every gang member had his hand in the air!"

John turned them over to a local church ministry, and the last he heard, they were still being discipled by that same church.

When we know who we are in Christ, we take delight in sharing with other people who they can be in Christ.

Jesus saw a constant adventure in others. When the men came screaming out of the tombs with long, scraggly beards and foam pouring out of their mouths, Jesus said, "This is going to be an adventure." An adventure is in store for each of us when we reach out to others! I want that for my life, don't you? I do not want merely to exist and spend my entire life locked in a church closet. I hope that is true of you, too.

THIRTEEN

The Adventure of Giving

I have held many things in my hands, and I have lost them all; but whatever I have placed in God's hands, that I still possess.

—MARTIN LUTHER

THERE IS A remarkable trend among today's ultra-rich people. In recent years, the world's most notable tycoons have been giving away huge amounts of money. Cable television mogul Ted Turner promised $1 billion to the United Nations. Microsoft founder Bill Gates, asserting that he will give away most of his fortune, has already endowed his foundation with $17 billion.

Even those who just recently made their fortune in Silicon Valley are already turning their attention, and pocketbooks, toward charitable causes. The founder of one popular Internet site gave away $5.7 million in one year. Another CEO gave away $20 million.[1]

Why do they do it? Is it because they don't know how to spend it all? That undoubtedly has something to do with it. But I think there is a more fundamental reason: After all the success, building billion-dollar companies and changing the face of commerce, they have found their lives lack adventure. Giving money away is, to them, the final frontier. To give away money is to invite adventure.

This is especially true for the follower of Christ who gives his money in obedience to God. In the past few years I have seen more miracles that involve giving than ever before in my ministry. The Dream Center has been a miracle of giving. We started out with only a dream and absolutely no money.

Let me share some of the remarkable adventures of giving we have encountered along the way.

FROM ONE BUILDING FUND TO ANOTHER

David Cronc, pastor of Vaca Valley Christian Life Center in Vacaville, California, came to our Pastors' School. His church had recently established a fund in order to raise enough money to build an auditorium seating 2,500 people. While David was with us, he had a little extra time on his hands, so he decided to go up to prayer mountain behind our church to pray. There he sensed God telling him, "Go home to your congregation and ask them to give the $117,00 in your building fund to the Dream Center."

After the Pastors' School was over, David returned to his church and shared with his congregation what he had sensed in prayer the previous week. "I feel we ought to give all our building fund money to the Dream Center, but we will not give it to them unless every one of you who gave agrees to it." He took a vote, and everyone in the church agreed. With that, the church gave the Dream Center $117,000—the church's entire building fund.

Shortly thereafter, a man from the church approached Rev. Crone and said, "I think it's time to get the building project going again, so here's what I'll do. For every dollar our people give to the church building fund, I will match it with another dollar."

When the matching gift offer was announced, money began pouring into the church. The last time I checked, they had more money in their building fund than they had to begin with, and they were nearing completion of their building project. God blesses obedience!

Miracles From Unexpected Sources

The first year Jentezen Franklin began serving as pastor at his church in Gainesville, Georgia, he attended our Pastors' School. Dramatically affected by our meetings, he returned to Gainesville ready to do all he could to win souls.

Pastor Franklin began a bus ministry and a Master's Commission program, and he preached illustrated sermons. In short, he did everything he could to build a great church.

When Jentezen invited me to preach at his church, I told him the offering taken would go to the Dream Center. I preached, and his people gave $50,000 for the Dream Center!

A week later he stood up on a Sunday morning and said, "I just found out that a piece of property across the street that we desperately need is available. We need an offering of approximately $500,000 to buy that property." So they received an offering that morning.

Following the service a couple he had never met walked up to him. They owned the Malibu Race Tracks, and they told him, "We will give half of the amount you need if the church will match it." God gave them the entire miracle. To this day, Jentezen says he believes it happened because they gave that $50,000 the week before to the Dream Center.

MIRACLES FROM ALL SIDES

Sam Carr, an upbeat and all-around fun guy, pastors the Word of Life Center in Shreveport, Louisiana. God placed in his heart a desire to purchase a television station for Shreveport—one that would reach half a million people. He made his application to the FCC, filed his papers and obtained a promise for a UHF-TV station. It was literally a dream come true. His people were excited, and Sam was convinced God wanted him to preach the gospel over the airwaves. Now he would have his own station.

Sam soon discovered that filing the papers was the easy part. Getting the station on the air required at least $1 million dollars because they had to complete the construction of the station before the license expired. A local bank assured the church that they would be able to negotiate a loan. On the day the loan was to be completed, Sam and his attorney entered a large room in the bank with an endlessly long conference table. At one end sat the bank officers. Sam and his attorney took their seats at the other.

The executive vice president stood and, in his best banker tone, told Sam that they were willing to loan the money for a church building, but they would not issue the loan in order to put Word of Life's Christian television station on the air.

His holy ire rising, Sam stood up and proclaimed in no uncertain terms that nothing would keep them from putting their television station on the air. They had never been late on any church debt payments and, by hook or by crook, the television station would proceed. Sam left, stunned by the proceedings. The bank never called back.

At the same time, the city decided to confiscate twenty-tree acres of the church's land close to the municipal airport, prohibiting the church from constructing any buildings or roads. The change left the church with no room to expand, no additional area for parking and little access. For two years the church skirmished with the city in court. The church was being drained, financially and spiritually. Thousands of dollars were spent in litigation as they struggled to complete the building of their television station before their license expired.

In the middle of the difficult circumstances Sam received a phone call from a group of investors offering to loan the church money for the television station. On his twenty-fifth wedding anniversary Sam flew out of town to meet them and work out the details. He was to return in time for the celebration the church had planned. But by eight o'clock that evening he was forced to call with the disappointing news that his meeting was lasting longer than expected, and he would have to miss the event. His one consolation as he boarded the plane home was that he held the loan check in his hand.

The next morning the *Wall Street Journal* published an article about a company indicted by the FCC for fraud. The men named were the signers of Sam's cherished check. His deal collapsed, and floodgates of trouble broke loose.

Finally, the television station went on the air. The church was still fighting the city in court regarding the zoning laws.

Three months later I was invited to speak at Word of Life's annual Freedom Crusade. As Sam and I renewed our acquaintance, we swapped stories about the hassles we were dealing with in our respective ministry fronts.

That night at church I shared the vision God had given me for the Dream Center. When I was done, Sam felt led to take up an offering to help us with our project. When Sam filled in the check for the Dream Center following the service, inwardly he thought, *We need the money more than they do. We're barely meeting our expenses.* But in obedience, he handed me the check for $33,000.

Giving an amount of that magnitude required an act of faith—an act of faith that activated future miracles. Soon after that the city contacted Sam and said they wanted to settle. They returned the land they had taken to the church and let them keep the money the city had paid them for it. That paid the attorney fees and $50,000 of their out-of-pocket expenditures. The city had even cleared the land, which would have cost upwards of $100,000.

However, the television station had been losing money. Even though reputable organizations and churches had purchased time, the station's receivables were extensive. I hate to tell you this, but preachers and ministries tend to be slow to pay.

In September a call came from a gentleman who wanted to talk about purchasing the station. Sam replied, "It's not for sale." In the informal conversation the man asked what the church would take for the station. Sam knew it was worth about $2 million, but he answered, "Five million dollars." Undaunted, the man said he would get back to Sam.

Soon thereafter, the businessman returned with a message from his investors. Their offer was $3.8 million—cash! In addition, they would place in the contract a provision stating that Word of Life had the rights to twice the airtime the church was already using—free of charge. With plans to upgrade the station and double its power, Word of Life would be able to reach more people over the airwaves than they had ever dreamed of.

Suddenly, bills were paid and enough money was available to build a new sanctuary with cash. But that's not all. Earlier, the church had acquired a permit to run a small radio station. The station itself, however, had never been developed. A man contacted the church and paid them $400,000 for the permit.

All the while, Sam Carr and Word of Life Center continued planting seeds into the Dream Center.

> Now may He who supplies seed to the sower, and bread for food, supply and multiply the seed you have sown and increase the fruits of your righteousness, while you are enriched in everything for all liberality, which causes thanksgiving through us to God.
> —2 CORINTHIANS 9:10–11

When we give sacrificially into the kingdom of God, heaven and earth are activated to move on our behalf. That's what makes giving an adventure. We give out of our need, and then we watch to see how God blesses our giving.

For years I have taught emphatically that our giving to

the cause of Christ should be motivated by love, not by the expectation of immediate rewards. I have tended to be critical of those who preached sowing and reaping for return. But through the experience of the Dream Center, I have seen new indications that I may have missed a principle of the blessings God's people receive when they unselfishly share their resources. Adventuring yourself in giving invites miraculous provision.

FOURTEEN

The Adventure of Living Beyond Safe

Great deeds are usually wrought at great risks.

—HERODOTUS

IN 1910, A young lady named Lillian Trasher stepped off a ship on the shores of Egypt. She was single, the daughter of educated Southerners, and she showed a special talent in art and design. But God had planted an adventure in her heart that drew her away from the safety of a career in America to the uncertain sands of this Middle Eastern country. Though her parents were not Christians, Lillian had accepted the Lord at a young age, and when she reached her twenties she felt a call to the foreign mission field. "Lord," she said, "if there is anything You want me to do, I'll do it."

And she meant it.

The Lord impressed on her heart the continent of Africa.

The impression was so strong that she broke off her engagement to a young man and began looking for ways to go to Africa. When certain individuals learned of her determination, money came in for her to go to Egypt. She arrived there with seventy dollars and no promise of support. Egypt was to be her home for the next fifty-one years.

She traveled to a town along the Nile River called Assiout where a group of missionaries lived. Lillian discovered that poverty drove down the value of human life. She was moved one day when she came upon a dying mother and a starving infant in a wretched little hut by the Nile. The mother begged Lillian to take care of the baby while some of the mother's relatives said they ought to just throw the child into the river. Appalled, Lillian took the child home to care for it.

God immediately began sending her more children, and soon she gained a reputation for accepting the unwanted. She founded an orphanage in the middle of that Muslim country to teach, feed, house and clothe youngsters who had lost one or both of their parents. By the time she died in 1961, ten thousand children had grown up in her care. They called her "Mama Lillian," and her orphanage gained the favor of the entire country, even though she was a Christian and unashamedly taught her "children" the Word of God.

Today, the Lillian Trasher Orphanage is considered one of the most important institutions in Egypt, responsible for saving a generation from death and destitution. Some of Mama Lillian's children hold important positions in Egyptian universities and in the government. More than twenty thousand children to date have graduated from the orphanage. Every year at their annual open house, governors and high dignitaries laud Mama Lillian for her example.

All this from a young woman who left the shores of America with no guarantee of safe return (and indeed, she never did return except to raise money on a handful of occasions). Lillian Trasher discovered the adventure of living beyond safe. Her life bears the fingerprints of God.[1]

Safe and good. Some of us want a nice, safe, cuddly God we can parade in front of others. On Sunday morning we dress Him up and show Him off. This handy-dandy Jesus fits neatly into our pocket so we can take Him with us to officiate at dinnertime prayers, Thanksgiving celebrations, invocations or wherever needed.

When He becomes an inconvenience, He goes back into our pocket until the next time He may be of use. He doesn't convict us, challenge us, rebuke us or chasten us. This God doesn't dabble in our personal matters, and He never asks us to take risks or leaps of faith. This Jesus is a nice, dignified, respectable Man who died to help others become nice, dignified, respectable people.

Is this your picture of God?

C. S. Lewis's well-known children's book, *The Lion, the Witch and the Wardrobe,* tells a story involving a mysterious lion named Aslan, who is a symbol of Christ. At one point in the tale, Mr. Beaver describes Aslan the mighty lion to Lucy. Lucy asks, "Is he—quite safe?"

"Safe?" Mr. Beaver replies. "Who said anything about safe? 'Course he isn't safe. But he's good. He's the King, I tell you."[2]

The discourse between Mr. Beaver and Lucy reveals two equally opposing views concerning the nature of God and adventure. Christians, for the most part, see God as either "safe and good" or "not safe, but good."

Not safe, but good. In the Gospels, especially the

Gospel of John, we see Jesus constantly on the run because His detractors were pursuing Him with the intent of taking His life. Undoubtedly He was good: He healed the sick, fed the hungry and even raised the dead. But "safe" wouldn't exactly describe Jesus.

He worked miracles on the Sabbath in violation of the religious laws of His day. He challenged the practices of the Pharisees. And He had the audacity to drive the money-changers out of the Temple courts. Also, Jesus was not one to shy away from controversy.

On the other hand, this Jesus is not so unsafe or so unpredictable that He cannot be trusted. Because He is good and because He is the king, Jesus is ultimately dependable.

As Christ's followers, we are not called to be safe either. Good, yes, but safe, no. Dependable, yes; predictable, no. Let's not make any mistakes: There is a danger in serving God and giving ourselves to others. It cost Jesus His life. It may very well cost us ours.

Moving Away From the Safety Net

In my book *Dream Again,* I shared the story of a homeless man who gave his life to Christ and then brought his brother, Jack Wallace, to our church. Jack later became one of our pastors.

As God blessed Jack's ministry at Phoenix First Assembly, we began sensing God might be opening the door for him to pastor a church of his own. An invitation came for Jack to take a church in inner-city Detroit, so I blessed my son in the faith and released him.

The congregation Jack agreed to pastor was in a state of

brokenness and division. Dissension was tearing the people apart. In the previous five years, three pastors had come and gone, each starting ministries within a six-mile radius of the church. Fueling the church's problems were a controlling board and a general lack of direction. People who could have otherwise helped push the church back up to God's higher ground of blessing began jumping ship. Compounding the problem: Despite their location in the ethnically based inner city, the congregation was 95 percent white.

The Wallaces moved from the "safety net" of Phoenix into a church that could be described as a Mack truck sliding hopelessly down a muddy hill.

At the onset, about two hundred met in a small sanctuary. Sunday night attendance was sparse, and just six people attended the first Wednesday prayer meeting! In a few short years, however, the church exploded. Communicating a much broader vision than before, their name has been changed to Detroit World Outreach.

Looking around the congregation on a Sunday morning reveals a truly integrated church. Racial reconciliation is at work. Children's ministries and bus ministries are penetrating places formerly presumed impenetrable. Satellite churches are spreading the gospel throughout greater Detroit.

During this time, Jack was stabbed eighteen times. Making a difference in drug-infested neighborhoods may mean facing danger. Jack could have easily reacted to his injuries by saying, "Here I am, trying to help these people, and they treat me like this? Forget it! I won't risk my family for this."

Jack realizes the danger. But when our focus is on Jesus, we don't give up. Today, Jack pastors one of the largest

Assemblies of God churches in the nation. Though he has seen danger, he has also experienced blessing.

How often do we want the fruit of our labor without the labor? We want immediate gratification without sacrifice. We want the thrill of victory without risking the agony of defeat. But with every adventure also comes the danger. Here's how Scripture describes the great adventurers of the faith:

> And what more shall I say? For the time would fail me to tell of Gideon and Barak and Samson and Jephthah, also of David and Samuel and the prophets: who through faith subdued kingdoms, worked righteousness, obtained promises, stopped the mouths of lions, quenched the violence of fire, escaped the edge of the sword, out of weakness were made strong, became valiant in battle, turned to flight the armies of the aliens. Women received their dead raised to life again.
>
> Others were tortured, not accepting deliverance, that they might obtain a better resurrection. Still others had trial of mockings and scourgings, yes, and of chains and imprisonment. They were stoned, they were sawn in two, were tempted, were slain with the sword. They wandered about in sheepskins and goatskins, being destitute, afflicted, tormented—of whom the world was not worthy.
>
> —HEBREWS 11:32–38

Adventure vacations and extreme sporting events look like small potatoes when compared to what these men and women of faith went through. What determines whether people are adventurers in the kingdom of God or not? I believe it is how they respond to danger—whether they give up or dig deeper and try harder.

TAKING A DANGEROUS STAND FOR RIGHTEOUSNESS

When our church in Davenport took a stand against pornography and massage parlors, not only did we face vocal opposition, but our lives were in danger as well. We politely told the store owners that if they were going to display their pornography in public, we would be forced to take our business elsewhere. We passed out tracts to the massage parlor customers, effectively shutting down their businesses. Then we asked the city council to prohibit public displays of pornography and to outlaw all massage parlors.

Because the massage parlors were owned by the mob in Chicago, they sent a man to town to intimidate us. Death threats began arriving in the mail. Calls came in to our church office claiming that bombs had been placed in our building. For a while I was encouraged to wear a flak jacket (a bullet protective vest) while I preached on Sunday mornings.

When our church refused to relent, the mob focused on my family. Pictures were sent to my home detailing what they were going to do to my wife if they caught her. The lives of my children were endangered as well. Because our family was in danger, we were under twenty-four-hour police protection. I've never lived so close to the Lord as I did then!

In the end, the sale of pornography was curtailed in Davenport, and the massage parlors were closed. Five young women from the massage parlor even visited our church to see how mean I was and ended up giving their lives to Christ.

Do I regret the experience? Not on your life! During those moments of danger I never felt the presence of almighty God so strongly.

In 1992 I returned to the city and the church I had pastored thirteen years earlier. That morning I opened up the *Quad City Times* newspaper, only to be greeted by an article written by columnist Bill Wundram. The headline read, "Here's-s-s-s Tommy!" —just like the old *The Tonight Show* with Johnny Carson. He shared his regrets in seeing our family move to Phoenix, and then he reflected on some of the highlights of my eight-year stay in Davenport. He went on to write:

> When Tommy came to Davenport, Westside had 75 members. When the spellbinder left, it had a membership of 5,000, and he had chased sin and the devil and had closed the city's plethora of porno parlors, and religion has perhaps never been the same.[2]

Mr. Wundram's comments, coming from a local newspaper, left me feeling that we really made a difference in our city.

The danger was great, but never was the fruit so sweet!

My life has been threatened other times as well. At our Easter pageant a few years ago we hosted seven thousand people a night for two weeks in our sanctuary. One night, just as the lights went down, a man at the wheel of a van charged across the grass area and drove the van through the double doors. Then he backed up and tried to go through the sanctuary doors onto the platform to run me over. Somehow, some men caught him before he did. The man was sentenced to prison, and just before he got out of prison he left death threats for me. He said he would come get me the Sunday after he was released, but my ushers were ready for him.

He never came. I told the church later in jest that I was glad no one came down the aisle early to get saved at that service, or my ushers would have tackled him.

There is always danger. As I write this, the memory of the shooting in the Baptist church in Ft. Worth is still fresh in my memory. The Columbine shootings, the Paducah shootings, all involved born-again believers on the adventure of faith being attacked by the enemy. Some people hate the work of God. Every Christian should understand that.

THE FOUR PAINS OF AN ADVENTURER

Prospective adventurers cross my path on a regular basis. I meet pastors and church leaders who sincerely desire to build great churches for the glory of God. Many attend conferences on church growth. They know the ins and outs of effective churches, but still their churches don't grow. Why not? When it comes to applying what they have learned, they are unwilling to suffer the pain of multiplication.

Every adventurer must accept the possibility of danger and pain. Counting the cost before setting out on any adventure is crucial. Jesus said in Luke 14 that before any person begins constructing a tower, he or she must first determine the cost to build it. Every adventure is fraught with possible pain. In addition to physical pain, four other pains potentially jeopardize every adventure:

The pain of relationships

As long as you stay in your box, people will be happy with you. But when you grow impatient with the constraints of that little box and you break free, your closest allies may become your greatest enemies.

Maintaining the status quo never intimidated anyone. In fact, most people prefer the status quo because the success of others exposes the impotence of their own ways. Some pastors will never experience everything God has for them because they're afraid that their peers will become jealous of them. The need for acceptance by their colleagues is greater than their desire for success and effectiveness.

Pursuing God's adventure may also risk your relationships with other people in your church. Fellow believers may be unable to grasp your vision and may pull away or even leave. They may be unwilling to put in the effort or the finances required to operate the kind of ministry you envision. Leadership is often intimidated by new ideas, because if an idea becomes successful, it will expose the leadership's own ineffectiveness. Most Christians are content with the status quo because the status quo requires little of them and, above all, presents little danger.

The pain of misunderstanding

People ahead of their time are usually misunderstood and misinterpreted. By forging ahead into unexplored territory, they risk unfair judgment and accusation.

There was a time when I was back in Iowa that everybody laughed at us for busing in the poor children of our community. They used to say, "All Barnett has are the little bus kids and some poor people nobody else wants." And you know, that is about all we had. But God used those precious little children to light our hearts on fire for the gospel. Those poor little children grew up learning how to apply biblical principles of stewardship and responsibility, and they ended up becoming devoted, committed, generous adult members.

Some of those same pastors who criticized me years ago are now involved in the very ministry they so vehemently opposed. What matters most to me is not that they acknowledge I was right but that they share the gospel with the poor and hurting.

The pain of loneliness

Because of the risk involved and the propensity for misunderstanding, adventures rarely include more than one or two people. As a result, loneliness becomes a legitimate concern.

After going through the "Faith Hall of Fame" with its adventurers and the perils they faced, the writer of Hebrews concludes by exhorting the reader:

> Let us run with endurance the race that is set before us, looking unto Jesus, the author and finisher of our faith, who for the joy that was set before Him endured the cross, despising the shame, and has sat down at the right hand of the throne of God.
>
> —HEBREWS 12:1–2

In other words, when you encounter the pain of misunderstanding and loneliness, focus on Jesus Christ and not on the people who desert you, misunderstand you or malign you. Which brings me to the next pain of an adventurer . . .

The pain of criticism

Most people despise two things: success and failure. And they probably hate success more than failure. Read almost any newspaper or magazine and you will find articles and exposés indicting the characters of people who try to make a difference. Something within our human nature makes us feel vindicated when a successful individual fails. Adventurers will always be criticized: Joseph was an adventurer who was mocked by his brothers. Nehemiah was an adventurer who faced ridicule when he rebuilt the wall in Jerusalem.

A man came to his pastor one day and confessed, "Pastor, you have to help me. I'm so full of despair. I'm depressed and burdened."

The pastor looked at the man and asked, "Is it dark where you are? Is it gloomy? Is it cloudy and misty?"

"Yes, yes, yes," he replied.

The pastor jumped up, ran around the desk and shouted, "Praise God! You are where the lilies bloom. It's in that dark and gloomy atmosphere that lilies flourish." God performs His deepest work in our lives not in our triumphs, but in our moments of sorrow and pain.

Living beyond safe may mean exposing ourselves to hardship, but God can use the pain we endure to establish a work greater than ourselves. God may not be safe, but He is ultimately good. And because He is good, any pain we face He will use for an even greater good if we let Him.

FIFTEEN

The Adventure of Wanting to Quit

Never give in! Never give in! Never! Never! Never! Never!
In anything great or small, large or petty—never give in
except to convictions of honor and good sense.

—SIR WINSTON CHURCHILL

JEREMY CAME FROM a long line of distinguished preachers. This up-and-coming minister rose to prominence in his early twenties and served as a spiritual advisor in the courts of four successive kings.

At the beginning of his ministry he assisted the king in implementing religious reforms in his nation. Unfortunately, the king was assassinated before the reforms were complete. One of the king's sons ascended to the throne, but he was not interested in serving God. Attempting to continue the earlier reforms, Jeremy desperately tried to convince the new king to continue where his father had left off, but his pleas went unheeded. As a result, Jeremy had quite a tempestuous relationship with the king, as well as with the next two kings.

Jeremy experienced many of the pains only an adventurer would understand: His relationships suffered for the stands he took, he was frequently misunderstood, he had few friends and he was often criticized for what he said. Because of his radical message of complete surrender to God, he lived in constant conflict. His life was threatened by fellow ministers, he was publicly humiliated and at one point was thrown into a muddy cistern to die.

Although he warned his beloved people that unless they returned to God, they would fall, his warnings were ignored. Yet, he remained faithful to God's call on his life. Even today in his writings one can sense his deep love for his people and a heartfelt desire to see his people turned back to God. Eventually his prophecies came true, and his people were taken into captivity by a greater nation. During his nation's collapse, this young adventurer was tempted to quit. Why risk his neck for a stiff-necked people? Here is his answer:

> For when I spoke, I cried out;
> I shouted, "Violence and plunder!"
> Because the word of the LORD was made to me
> A reproach and a derision daily.
> Then I said, "I will not make mention of Him,
> Nor speak anymore in His name."
> But His word was in my heart like a burning fire
> Shut up in my bones.
> I was weary of holding it back,
> And I could not.

Who was this minister? Who said he wanted to quit but couldn't? His name wasn't Jeremy but Jeremiah, and his words about fire in his bones are recorded in Jeremiah 20:8–9.

THE HALL OF PEOPLE WHO WANTED TO QUIT

Christians tend to idealize the lives of men and women in spiritual leadership. They comment, "That evangelist is superhuman," or "That pastor must be a spiritual giant." But my goal in this chapter is to tear down any false conceptions you might have.

In my travels I spend time with many prominent spiritual leaders. Someone once commented to me, "Spending time with such great men and women of God must bless you and inspire you." But I answered, "No, what inspires me is not their greatness, but their humanity. Their failures inspire me because if God can use them, He can use me as well."

The danger and pain of an adventure can exact a toll on a person over time. In the passage above we find a prophet who was quite discouraged. In fact, he wanted to quit the ministry and get a little cabin on a lake so he could spend all day fishing. But the Word of God burned in his bones like a fire, and he couldn't hold it in. Jeremiah wanted to quit. But if you read the annals of the great men and women of God, you will find that Jeremiah was not alone. Allow me to name some prominent men of God who wanted to quit.

Abraham was called *the friend of God,* but when a famine struck and the economy went south, he left the land of promise and moved to Egypt. By leaving the Promised Land, he also risked forsaking God's blessing.

Moses grew so frustrated with the complaints of the children of Israel, he asked God to take his life (Num. 11:15). Elijah, on the heels of the greatest triumph in his ministry, ran in terror into the wilderness to evade the pursuit of Queen Jezebel's henchmen. He cried out to God, "It is enough! Now, LORD, take my life, for I am no better than my fathers!" (1 Kings 19:4).

It bears mentioning that Moses and Elijah were the two most prominent figures in Israel's recorded history, yet they both encountered periods of deep discouragement and times when they wanted to quit.

Peter, who walked on the water, returned to his fishing business after denying Jesus three times before seeing Him crucified. In fact, each one of the disciples except John forsook Jesus at the cross and fled.

Martin Luther nailed the 95 Theses on the Wittenburg Door and stood up to the Catholic church during a time of great corruption. His vision of the grace of God sparked the Reformation and a time of great renewal in the church. Yet history tells us this bold man struggled with discouragement and severe depression, many times wanting to quit.

Charles Haddon Spurgeon, the "Prince of Preachers," the man who built the great church in London at age eighteen, struggled with depression as well. During his bouts of discouragement, he begged God to release him from his responsibilities.

It may surprise you to know that I have wanted to quit. When I moved to Davenport, Iowa, I encountered the seventy-six meanest Christians I had ever met in my life. I called my dad and said, "I must be out of God's will. These members are resistant to change. People aren't getting saved. I just want to move back to Kansas City."

My father replied, "Son, if you are going to go home, crawl out of the city in a sewer." In other words, the sewer goes out under the city, and I'd have to crawl out in shame. I decided that I didn't want to do that, so I didn't quit.

Jesus Himself wanted to quit. The night He was betrayed, Jesus went to the Garden of Gethsemane. In deep distress He prayed, "Father, if it is Your will, take this cup away from Me; nevertheless not My will, but Yours, be done" (Luke 22:42). In other words, Jesus was saying, "God, I don't want to go to the cross. I *want* to quit, but doing Your will is more important than that."

THE THREE REDEEMING QUALITIES OF WANTING TO QUIT

Common to every person who has ever lived—including Jesus—is the desire to give up. And that's not all bad. In fact, there are three redeeming qualities about wanting to quit.

Redeeming Quality #1: Wanting to quit is a sign of success.

Successful people are the only ones who can quit because they have something *to* quit. For example, a young couple decides to enroll in our Pastors College. They sell their home, get rid of the dog they love, pack all their belongings into an old, broken-down car and move to Phoenix. Once they arrive, they meet strange people and enter an unfamiliar environment. Eventually they get discouraged from the difficult transition, and they quit.

Of course, I recommend against quitting. Yet I have

more respect for people who at least try than those who don't. So having something to quit is actually an indicator of success.

Some time ago, I drove by an abandoned housing development. Scattered throughout the property were the remnants of meandering concrete foundations and half-finished houses. In the middle stood a house that had been completed at one time, but then burned. I decided I would rather be a house that burned than a house that had never been built. At least the burned house served its purpose for a time. The others never fulfilled the purpose for which they were started.

In the same way, I have more respect for the person who falls than the one who never tries. I get impatient with folks who stay on the ground and shoot down others who attempt to fly.

Redeeming Quality #2: The more you have to quit, the more you want to quit.

The higher you go, the more frightening the journey becomes, and the more there is to leave behind if you quit. Jesus said, "For everyone to whom much is given, from him much will be required" (Luke 12:48). People who have been given more are held to a higher standard. And because they have more to give, they also have more to give up.

God has blessed me far greater than I deserve. It is my privilege to pastor two of America's many great churches. Because of God's blessing, I believe the intensity of my desire to quit is greater than that of the pastor of a church of one hundred. Why? Because I have more to quit.

Not only am I responsible for preaching three sermons a

week in Phoenix, but the buck stops with me whenever our church deals with problems and controversies. As senior pastor I must keep abreast of the needs of the fifteen thousand people attending my church as well as oversee the associate pastors who pastor them on a day-to-day basis.

My congregation has released me to speak at conferences and in churches around the country during the week. I also spend at least two days a week four hundred miles away in Los Angeles at the Dream Center. One of my responsibilities there is to oversee a budget of $350,000 per month at the Dream Center and find creative ways to make up the difference if there is a shortfall. Last, but certainly not least, our congregation recently planted a new church in Scottsdale, which I pastor as well.

With such a full plate, I have plenty to quit. I have discovered that the higher I rise, the scarier the ride becomes. And colder. And lonelier. And more dangerous. And riskier.

Redeeming Quality #3: You can enjoy the luxury of wanting to quit if you know that you are not going to quit.

Did you know you can be a wanna-be quitter without being a quitter? You can enjoy the luxury of wanting to quit if you know you are not going to quit.

How do I know I am not going to quit? Because I have never quit. When a man applies for a loan, how does the loan company know that he will pay it off? Because he has a track record of paying his bills. Past performance is usually a pretty good indicator of future results.

Since I have never quit, it doesn't worry me when I *want* to quit. I can say to myself, *I would just like to quit,* without worrying because I know that I am not going to quit.

Countless people begin an adventure, then when they face danger and pain greater than they think they can bear, they proclaim, "I just want to quit." And they do.

I wanted to quit the first church I pastored. I wanted to quit when my life and the lives of my family were threatened while we fought the massage parlors in Davenport. I wanted to quit when a group of Muslims warned me they'd kill me if I didn't stop defending Israel. I wanted to quit when *The (Arizona) Republic* and the *Wall Street Journal* criticized me after the fall of some well-known Assemblies of God pastors. I wanted to quit my walk across the desert when my feet hurt so badly I thought I would faint from the pain. But I knew I was not going to quit because I'm not a quitter! Therefore, I can have the luxury of wanting to quit.

I am so opposed to quitting that I have literally cut the word out of every dictionary I own. It does not belong in there for a child of the living God! There is nothing wrong with saying you want to quit, just as long as you don't.

THREE METHODS TO KEEP YOURSELF FROM QUITTING

Perhaps you don't have the luxury of being able to say, "I have never quit anything." Here are three ways to keep yourself from quitting next time.

Method #1: Burn every bridge so you can't go back.

Live in such a way that you have nothing else to do if you quit. Our two churches are so far out in left field that we couldn't go back to where we were if we wanted. We prayed, "O God, find us a new building to house the

Dream Center." We fasted and prayed, and then God gave us a building greater than our wildest dreams. Now we pray, "O God, You got us into this mess. Now You need to supply a way to pay the bills every month." Every miracle necessitates another miracle. At this point, we couldn't go back if we wanted to.

Method #2: Don't tell anyone you want to quit.

Just because you're thinking about quitting doesn't mean you have to say it. You can tell people afterward, but not while you're struggling with completing the job. All too often our friends assist us in following through with our wishes.

Method #3: Don't expose yourself to what you do not want to be.

People tell me, "Pastor, I may not agree with what that church believes, but I go there because I like their worship." Eventually they not only approve of the church's worship, but of their doctrine as well. We all become that to which we expose ourselves. If we expose ourselves to the values that most television programs portray, we will eventually become like them. If we feed our minds with books that encourage us to seek our own self-fulfillment, we will become concerned only with ourselves. If we spend an inordinate amount of time around people who quit, we will become quitters.

TWO REASONS WHY YOU CAN'T QUIT

Never before has it been so important for us to remain faithful in even the little things. Here are two reasons why it is imperative that believers not quit.

Reason #1: You can't quit because Jesus said not to.

"No one, having put his hand to the plow, and looking back, is fit for the kingdom of God" (Luke 9:62). Whatever ministry God has called you to—salaried or volunteer, ordained or lay—you can never quit.

Scripture says, "For the gifts and the calling of God are irrevocable" (Rom. 11:29). People often interpret this verse to mean that God will never remove His gifts and callings from us. But that's only partly true. We also bear the responsibility of using those gifts. Quitting runs contrary to kingdom principles.

Reason #2: You can't quit because you hold the future in your hands.

Every action, reaction and non-action you take has broad implications for the people who follow in your footsteps.

We can't afford to quit because our children are watching. Over time, children become a reflection of their parents. When we quit, they learn that quitting is a viable option. When we quit, we portray to them an impotent gospel, a cheap imitation of God's grace that is not powerful enough to overcome. I don't believe my three children would be living for Jesus Christ today if I had quit every time I felt like it.

When we fail or fall short, we get back up. The Bible tells us, "Though a righteous man falls seven times, he rises again, but the wicked are brought down by calamity" (Prov. 24:16, NIV). People made righteous through the blood of

Jesus Christ are able to rise again.

One New Year's Day in the Tournament of Roses parade, a beautiful float suddenly sputtered and quit because it ran out of gas. The whole parade was held up until someone could get a can of gas. The irony of the spectacle was that this float represented the Standard Oil Company. With its vast oil resources, its truck had run out of fuel.[1]

A Christian who quits is no different from that Standard Oil Company float. As believers in Jesus Christ, we are linked to the greatest power supply in the universe. We have no valid reason for running out of strength to finish what we start. When we quit, we communicate to the scores of onlookers around us, *I don't believe God's grace is great enough to carry me through.*

Jesus promised His followers that after Pentecost, they would be "endued with power from on high" (Luke 24:49). You may have good reason to *want* to quit, but you have no reason *to* quit because "He who has begun a good work in you will complete it until the day of Jesus Christ" (Phil. 1:6). And that's a promise from God!

You see, true adventurers are people who refuse to quit. Every week at the bottom of the staff report that my associate pastors turn in to me, I write these words, "Great men and women are ordinary people who just wouldn't quit."

I say the same thing to you: Don't ever quit.

SIXTEEN

The Adventure of Going a Little Farther

I will expect great things from God, and I will attempt great things for God.

—WILLIAM CAREY

WHILE SPEAKING AT a church conference, I agreed to participate in a question-and-answer session in which people could ask me anything—no holds barred. A man stood up and said, "Without wanting to offend you, I would like to ask you a question that has been puzzling me. I have studied and observed you for years, and I just don't understand the ministry of Tommy Barnett.

"There are great preachers—and you are a fine preacher—but I am sure there are greater preachers. You, I am sure, are a good organizer, but I know there are better organizers in the world. There are geniuses, and I am sure that you are probably not a genius. So, my question for you is, 'What makes the difference between your ministry and the ministry of other people? Why has God used you when there are greater and more gifted men God has not used to the same extent for His work?'"

Frankly, I was stumped. I just stood there shaking my head, not knowing what to say. I too have been amazed that God would use a vessel like me. Then a scripture came to me:

> Then Jesus came with them to a place called Gethsemane, and said to the disciples, "Sit here while I go and pray over there." And He took with Him Peter and the two sons of Zebedee, and He began to be sorrowful and deeply distressed. Then He said to them, "My soul is exceedingly sorrowful, even to death. Stay here and watch with Me."
> *He went a little farther* and fell on His face, and prayed.
>
> —MATTHEW 26:36–39, EMPHASIS ADDED

My thoughts instantly drifted back to the days when as a child, I would fall down, and my dad would say, "Get up and try it again." My father always went a little farther, and he raised me to go a little farther as well.

JESUS TAUGHT US TO GO A LITTLE FARTHER

Jesus' ministry embodied going just a little farther. He exhorted His followers, "If a man slaps you on the cheek, go a little farther—turn your head and let him slap the other cheek. If a man wants to take your shirt, go a little farther—give him your coat, too. If a man asks you to give him a ride somewhere, go a little farther—take him where he wants to go and then drive him to his next destination." (See Matthew 5:39–41.)

On the night of His betrayal Jesus was in deep distress. Most people in His shoes would have been distracted by the events about to take place, but Jesus went a little farther. In the waning hours of His life, Jesus knew He would be facing the greatest challenge of His earthly ministry, so He sought comfort, strength and direction in God's presence.

The kingdom of God moves forward on the shoulders of men and women who follow Jesus' example and go just a little farther. Perhaps that is the reason God has blessed me.

When I was in junior high, I tried out for the track team. It didn't take long before I discovered I wasn't fast enough to compete in the 60-yard dash. So I went a little farther and tried the 100-yard dash, but my time was still too slow. Then I tried the one-quarter mile, which was the longest distance run boys my age could to compete in, but still I wasn't fast enough.

My coach pulled me aside and said, "Tommy, maybe you should try running the hurdles. Speed is important, but good form is just as crucial. Most boys your age don't have the discipline to learn how to *step* over the hurdles rather than jump over them."

So day and night I practiced stepping rather than jumping over the hurdles. Though many of my opponents were faster runners than I was, I would beat them on the hurdles because I was stepping while they were jumping. Going a little farther than my competitors allowed me to continue running.

By the time I reached high school the rest of my competitors had learned how to combine speed with form.

Because I was a slow short distance runner, I was left behind. So I said to myself, "Maybe I'll just go a little farther and run the mile." I did well my freshman year, but my sophomore and junior year, again my competitors caught up with me.

I literally went a little farther and began running cross-country. At practice I ran as hard as the other boys, but then I would go home after school and run several more miles. I had learned to go a little farther. In hindsight I can see how God used my experience in long distance running to prepare me for my run from Phoenix to Los Angeles.

People who accomplish great things for God aren't necessarily the most gifted; they're simply the ones willing to go the second mile.

GOING A LITTLE FARTHER IN REACHING THE LOST

When I was sixteen I dedicated my life to the adventure of winning souls for Jesus Christ. In those days healing ministries were very popular. People responded to signs, wonders and miracles. But my primary calling was to win souls, so I made up my mind to preach to the unsaved. The only problem was, I didn't know how to get them to come to my meetings. Other men attracted crowds by preaching about prophecy, but most of the people who attended those meetings were already saved.

For the most part Christians weren't very good about inviting the unsaved, so I decided I would try to attract people by preaching illustrated messages. I built some hurdles and preached one message titled "Hurdling to Hell." For another illustrated sermon I gathered together a whip and a hammer, and then I built a cross.

The apostle Paul wrote, "I have become all things to all men, that I might by all means save some" (1 Cor. 9:22). Using all possible means at my disposal, I did what I could to find the most effective ways of winning the lost to Christ.

When I first began preaching, 16-millimeter movies were very popular, so I borrowed $5,000 from the bank and purchased a movie camera. Then, during my trip around the world, I stopped in Calcutta, India, and shot a missionary film titled *Mukti*, which means "freedom from bondage."

Much like an early documentary, *Mukti* showed the plight of people in desperate need of Jesus. Lurid displays of emaciated children, lepers, corpses being burned and dead babies thrown into the Ganges River all provided startling images of a world much different than America.

Upon my return to the United States, I went to Hollywood and edited the footage into what may have been one of the first religious films. By today's standards it may seem a bit gruesome, but in those days it was quite effective in attracting people who wouldn't normally come to church. Working with churches, we gave tickets away to friends, neighbors, coworkers—anyone we thought might be interested in seeing the film. Then at night, hundreds, sometimes thousands, would come to watch. When the film was over, I would preach and give an altar call. I decided I would do whatever it took to win the lost, and it took going a little bit farther.

When I became a pastor, I discovered once again people's reluctance to bring the unsaved to church. But I learned that kids were quite different. When they're enthusiastic about church, they'll bring everyone they know. So we tried different ways to draw kids in.

We built the world's biggest banana split. A wide, long gutter was placed on sawhorses in the church parking lot, then lined with bananas. Everyone from the church brought a gallon of ice cream to add to it. Then, after topping it off with pineapples, whipped cream, chocolate syrup, nuts and anything else we could think of, we turned the kids loose.

We also created a six-thousand-pound popsicle. The last I heard, Westside Assembly of God held a place in the *Guinness Book of World Records* for the world's biggest popsicle.

Following the apostle Paul's lead, we became all things to all men so that we might save some. We gave hamburgers to kids who came to church. We found out that once the kids started coming, their parents started coming, too. So we began developing outreaches that would appeal to the parents. We presented pageants, living Last Suppers and celebrations.

As God blessed our efforts in going a little farther, our success began generating criticism. We were denounced for having Johnny Cash sing. Others accused us of bribing children to come to church. Even my own denomination did not understand me. They called reaching kids "surface evangelism" or a "numbers game."

But I responded, "We count people because people count."

Moving to Phoenix, I continued where I left off at Westside Assembly. Today, we are the largest Assemblies of God church in America. Programmed into the psyche of our people is the desire to go a little farther in reaching the lost. We have Christmas and Easter musicals, which combined draw more than 225,000 people. An outdoor Fourth of July celebration draws 30,000 people annually.

GOING A LITTLE FARTHER AT THE DREAM CENTER

From the Dream Center's inception, Matthew and I decided to go a little farther than I had gone at Phoenix or Davenport to reach the people of our community with the gospel. While feeding the poor and ministering to the hurting on the streets have always been priorities, we chose to add some new approaches in ministry as well.

We started after-school teen counseling and Bible studies where teenagers who need help could find it. Any person interested in receiving a degree could do so through the intense study program of the Word of God in the L.A. Street University.

The majority of churches that play sports usually limit themselves to church leagues. We felt God calling us to go a little farther by starting a Tuesday night basketball league that attracts some of the top athletes in the city. Training in kickboxing and the discipline of martial arts self-defense is offered through the kickboxing ministry. Those who want to literally "get their feet wet" may do so through our surfing ministry.

The Los Angeles International Band presents the gospel through music every week. Every Wednesday, we offer a drama workshop in the theater where teenagers learn improvisation, staging, video, Christian comedy and other important theatrical techniques. From time to time guest actors teach.

Going a step farther means sharing the gospel in a way that is understandable and relevant. When it comes to trying out new ideas, we ask, *Why not?* rather than *Why?* That takes us to the next level. What is foremost in our minds is finding the world's greatest need and supplying it with the love of Jesus Christ.

Donald P. Jones once said, "The quickest and shortest way to crush whatever laurels you have won is for you to rest on them."[1] Going a little farther is the determination not to rest on your laurels. We find contentment in Jesus Christ, but we're never content to stay where we are.

I encourage the bus pastors in our bus ministry to tell themselves, "I will not be content with twenty-five people on my bus route. I want ninety or one hundred." We provoke our volunteers at the Dream Center to say, "We will not be content reaching 20,000 people a week at the Dream Center." Why not? Because people count. If we grow content with 20,000, what will happen to the person who would have been 20,001? Resting on our laurels could result in that person spending an eternity in hell.

In South America and Korea, many churches are running over 100,000 in attendance. Recently an official of my denomination challenged me, "We need a church that breaks that barrier in North America. I believe that church could be the Dream Center." I want to go a little farther to help that goal come to pass.

GOING A LITTLE FARTHER ONE STEP AT A TIME

The televangelist scandals of the late eighties changed the landscape of the American church. Failings in men I dearly love became headline news in papers across the country. Because of my association with these men, I became fodder for newspaper columns.

During those dark days there were times I didn't want to face the congregation. Every time I gave an altar call or received an offering, I worried about what people thought. During the week I dreaded facing pastors at the various conferences where I spoke. To be honest, during those difficult times, I didn't know how I was going to make it.

Through that experience, I learned that I don't need to say, "I have to endure this hardship for the rest of my life." All I need to say is, "I have to make it through today." People never finish races by saying, "I'm just going to finish." No, they win by declaring, "I am going to take this race one step at a time."

God guides us step by step. "The human mind plans the way, but the LORD directs the steps" (Prov. 16:9, NRSV). If He were to show us everything He has planned for us all at once, we would probably be so overwhelmed that we would give up even before we started.

During my walk across the desert when my legs were in pain and I felt like giving up, I said to myself, "I don't have to complete the whole run. All I need to do is complete the next step."

A farmer wanted to build a ten-mile fence around his huge farm, so he placed an ad in the paper. In no time a man inquired about what the job involved. The farmer replied, "I want you to build a ten-mile fence around my farm." The two men settled on the terms of the arrangement, and the man went to work. After only a few hundred feet, the man became discouraged because he realized how enormous the task was, so he quit.

The farmer placed another ad in the paper, and another man showed up and asked what the job was. The farmer answered, "I want you to take *three years* to build a ten-mile fence around my farm." The man went to work, but after only a few days, he became discouraged when he saw that he had only made a small dent in the project, so he quit.

A third time the farmer placed an ad in the paper, and a man showed up and asked what the job entailed. The farmer responded, "I want you to dig a hole here and put in a picket and dig another hole here and put in a picket, and just keep doing that." The fellow began building the fence and finished the ten-mile job.

You see, fences are not built in three years; they are built one picket at a time. Life is not lived by saying, "I am going to finish." Life is lived one day at a time, one step at a time.

Do you want to know how you can always be in the will of God? Be in the will of God today. And if you are in the will of God today, you will always be in the will of God.

Going a Little Farther Through Despair

I heard it once said, "Never despair, but if you do despair, work on undespairing." In other words, even when you feel despair, go just a little farther. That's what Jesus did in the Garden of Gethsemane.

After the children of Israel left the land of Egypt for the Promised Land, Pharaoh changed his mind about letting the people go. So he sent his army after the people of God, chasing them toward the Red Sea. Here was their dilemma: If they surrendered and returned to Egypt, conditions would be worse than they were before, and most of them would probably die from mistreatment. If they stayed where they were and fought, they would definitely be slaughtered. If they jumped into the Red Sea and tried to swim across, they would drown. What a choice!

Personally, when I die, I want to die going forward, doing what God has called me to do. The Israelites had no idea what God had planned, but because they determined to go a little farther and not go back, He parted the sea. God is looking for people who would rather drown than stay put or go backward. He is looking for people who would rather die than not move ahead.

During the war with Mexico in the 1840s, the American forces came under a fierce bombardment of cannon fire. With cannonballs landing all around them, soldiers begged their commander and future American president General Zachary Taylor to retreat. But General Taylor said, "We won't go back. We will go forward, and the cannonballs will fall behind us."

If you feel that you're under a barrage of enemy fire—whether it's coming from people or from the devil—just go a little farther, and the bullets will land behind you. There is a higher plane—onward, forward, marching toward the banner. Little is accomplished by those who look back. Jesus said, "No one, having put his hand to the plow, and looking back, is fit for the kingdom of God" (Luke 9:62).

YOU'RE NEVER TOO OLD FOR AN ADVENTURE

My father was an amazing man. He played baseball on the church team and led the league in hitting at age sixty-seven. As he got older, his legs began to give out, so the league established a rule especially for my dad that stated when a person turns sixty, he has the option of having somebody else run the bases for him. In fact, my father was so energetic that he pitched a double-header two days before he died. The entire league showed up at his funeral dressed in their baseball uniforms.

My dad is listed in the *Guinness Book of World Records* for the longest ongoing handball match. He met the same man for handball every week for over forty years.

When Rev. H. W. Barnett died, he left behind the legacy of an adventurer. Even as he grew older, he refused to give up the adventure. My desire is to follow in his footsteps.

As the North American populace becomes progressively older, people are learning that the adventure never has to end—not if they don't want it to end.

"You can tell a man is getting old depending on whether he looks at a sunrise or a sunset," said General Douglas MacArthur. Some people look at the sunset and reflect on adventures past. Because their best years are behind them, they slowly fade away into oblivion.

Other people wake up every morning, look at the rising sun and say, "I wonder what adventures are awaiting me today!" They are still hungry to go a little farther for the Lord. Age is a state of mind. As long as you have adventures to pursue, you slow down the aging process. Studies show that older people who remain active live longer. Plus, they enjoy life to a greater degree!

Scripture gives us portraits of great men and women who refused to allow their age to get in the way of the adventure God planned for them.

Abram (later known as Abraham) was seventy-five years old when he began his adventure and left Haran in search of the land of promise. When he was one hundred years old and his wife Sarah was ninety, two angels told them they were going to have a child—and they did!

Moses was eighty years old when he told Pharaoh, "Let my people go." Here's a description of Moses in his latter years: "Moses was one hundred and twenty years old when he died. His eyes were not dim nor his natural vigor diminished" (Deut. 34:7). How would you like to be described like that at one hundred twenty years of age?

Caleb was eighty years old when he first stepped into the Promised Land. Believing that his God could destroy the giants in the land, he gave a positive report to his superiors. Unfortunately, his fellow scouts didn't agree, so God made Israel wait another forty years until that entire generation died out before they went into the Promised Land.

Caleb and Joshua were the only men of their generation who were still alive forty years later because they were the only ones to believe their God was greater than their foes. By the time Caleb entered the Promised Land to stay, he was eighty-five. (See Joshua 14:10.) As a reward for his faithfulness, this adventurer was given Hebron as an inheritance, which still exists today.

Anna, a widow eighty-four years old, waited patiently and prayerfully in the temple courts for the Messiah to come. After witnessing the dedication of baby Jesus, this adventurous prayer warrior was free to die in peace. (See Luke 2:36–38.)

The apostle John was apparently the only one of the original twelve disciples to die of natural causes. Legend has it, though, that Emperor Domitian tried unsuccessfully to boil John in hot oil. Even at the age of sixty-five, John was still considered a threat to the Roman Empire.

But adventurers are not limited to Scripture.

Colonel Sanders was in his seventies when he began the Kentucky Fried Chicken restaurant chain. Before that he had gone bankrupt three times.

Mao Tse-Tung, the former chairman of the Communist Party in the People's Republic of China, was eighty years old when he swam across the Yellow River to celebrate his birthday. The stories of Chairman Mao and Colonel Sanders inspired me to begin my run across the desert at age sixty.

Following his term as president of the United States, George Bush parachuted out of an airplane. I read about a man who recently became a licensed physician—at fifty-five years of age.

Although I have already surpassed sixty years of age and qualify for an AARP card, I still have a running list of adventures I plan on achieving:

- Jumping out of an airplane
- Taking a bungee jump
- Making a hole in one
- Playing the great golf courses of the world
- Climbing Mt. Kilimanjaro
- Flying in a supersonic jet to Europe

I'm not afraid of growing old because I know that the adventure doesn't have to end prematurely. The prophet Joel foretold of the day when even old men would continue to dream:

> And it shall come to pass afterward that I will pour out My Spirit on all flesh; your sons and your daughters shall prophesy, your old men shall dream dreams, your young men shall see visions.
>
> —Joel 2:28

Old men dreaming dreams means there's still adventure left in their bones!

AN UNTAPPED RESOURCE FOR ADVENTURE

We live in the first generation of men who experience mid-life crises. But I believe I know the cure to old age and mid-life crises: have an adventure. Right now I'm so busy having adventures I don't have time to experience a mid-life crisis or even feel the effects of old age.

A man once said to me, "I'd like to see your scrapbook."

"I'm too busy right now making scrap," I answered back. I don't take pictures; I make memories.

The burgeoning population of senior citizens is using their expendable income to enjoy the pleasures resulting from a lifetime of saving and prosperity. But my challenge to retirees is this: Go a little farther than you have already gone. Rather than spend your money on golf carts and bus tours, why not adventure yourself one more time?

The older generation has untapped potential to make a difference today for the cause of Christ. Seasoned by a lifetime of experiences, they can invest themselves into the lives of our young people. With expendable income and a healthy pension, retirees can serve on the mission field or volunteer full time for a church or a ministry.

In his letter to a young pastor, the apostle Paul left for us the final words of an adventurer who refused to grow old:

> For I am already being poured out as a drink offering, and the time of my departure is at hand. I have fought the good fight, I have finished the race, I have kept the faith. Finally, there is laid up for me

the crown of righteousness, which the Lord, the righteous Judge, will give to me on that Day, and not to me only but also to all who have loved His appearing.

—2 TIMOTHY 4:6–8

Paul was a good starter. He planted churches all over the world. But he was also a good finisher. "I have finished the race."

Retiring from the adventure is like running a marathon but quitting just blocks short of the finish line. Don't quit before the end. Finish the race.

As you venture forward into God's adventure, whatever age you are, avoid becoming content. Anytime you simply maintain what you have, you begin to die. Go a little farther in using your creativity. Every year, raise the benchmark of your dreams, visions and goals.

The ocean has been explored, space has been explored, jungles and deserts have been explored. The only realm that remains unexplored is the realm of the Spirit of God. And it will forever remain virtually unexplored because it is unlimited. But explore one section at a time. Go a little farther in learning about God's principles and supernatural power. Go farther in learning the joy of giving so you can become an ever-increasing blessing in the kingdom of God.

As we commit ourselves to going just a little bit farther, we will discover God-sized adventures aren't impossible.

SEVENTEEN

Provoking Others to Adventure

Power lasts ten years; influence not more than a hundred.

—KOREAN PROVERB

LET ME ASK you a question: How is your provoker doing?

The word *provoke* is one of the most misunderstood words in the English language. When people hear that word, they usually think it means either causing someone to become angry ("Johnny, stop provoking your little sister!") or dressing in a way that causes someone to stumble (dressing provocatively).

However, *provoke* means "to sharpen, excite, stimulate or increase" what is already there. It means helping others to do and be the best they can. Provoking does not create new attributes, but it stimulates and accelerates what is already present within a person. For example, when I provoke someone to an adventurous lifestyle, I only stir up the dreams already resident within that person.

EARLY PROVOKERS

As a boy, I used to go out at night, gaze at the stars and wonder how far away they were. The morning star, the evening star, the Big Dipper and the Milky Way were all my friends. Staring into the heavens above I pondered, philosophized and dreamed of adventures to come. Much of my book *Portraits of Vision* was written in my mind as a little boy, even though it took many years before it was actually in print.

When I was a small boy, my father sat me on top of the pulpit and had me sing simple songs for the congregation. When I turned eight, he provoked me to learn the piano. The musical gifts I strengthened as a child benefited me greatly at the beginning of my ministry.

Our congregation in Davenport had already been designated the fastest-growing church in America. Then I went to hear Pastor Jack Hyles, a man of God who pastors the First Baptist Church of Hammond, Indiana, the largest church in America. As he roared out and challenged people to be all that they could be and to build great churches, I was provoked to go a little farther.

He told an unforgettable story about the first building his church built. Dr. Hyles operated as chief architect, contractor and decorator. When the building project was completed, the church held a dedication ceremony, and Dr. Hyles gave everyone a tour of the new facility. As people were exploring the new building, an architect asked him, "What kind of heating do you have in this building?"

"Heating?" Jack asked.

Somehow, in the busyness of the building project, he forgot to include a heating system in the plans. As a result, the brand-new building had to undergo major renovations to install a heating system even before it had been used. Jack Hyles provoked me to take action even when I lack the creative resources to get the job done. Sometimes you just have to "do it."

Earlier in my ministry in Phoenix, one morning at the conclusion of our service, Al Alexander, a new convert, came to me in tears. "Pastor," he said, "I would love to win souls as you do, but I don't know how. If you teach me how, I promise you that I will become a soulwinner, too." I had always been a soulwinner, but he provoked me to develop a new soulwinning program called "The Saturday Soulwinning Society" that is now used in churches around the world from Africa to Australia. Al Alexander did not make me a soulwinner, but he provoked me to be and do more of what I already was.

Prayer has always come naturally for me. Even as a boy, people in church would ask me, "Tommy, would you pray for me?" Many times I fell asleep on my knees praying for the needs of people in my father's congregation and later in mine.

But then I crossed paths with a man who spoke of prayer in a new fashion—prayer that could stop armies and change the course of nations. That man was Dr. David Yonggi Cho, pastor of Yoido Full Gospel Church in Seoul, Korea, the largest church in the world with over 750,000 people. He taught me that the key to their incredible growth is their commitment to prayer. In fact, their army of prayer warriors is bigger than the armies of some small nations! But Dr. Cho didn't teach me how to pray—he inspired me to pray more. And that is what the word *provoke* means.

WHAT IS YOUR PROVOKER DOING?

To a great extent, the person you are today is the result of the people who have provoked you in the past.

So I ask you, *What is your provoker doing? In what way are you provoking others?* You can provoke them to anger, to evil or jealousy. Or you can do as the Bibles tells us: "And let us consider how to *provoke* one another to love and good deeds" (Heb. 10:24, NRSV, emphasis added).

Do you provoke folks to love more? Do you provoke people to do more good? What qualities do you increase in others? You can provoke gossips to gossip, and critics to criticize. You can even provoke lazy people to become lazier. Everyone has a provoker, and everyone can use that provoker for good or bad. We all have a measure of good qualities and bad qualities that can also be stirred up in ourselves and that we can stir up in others.

Periodically I receive letters in the mail from pastors who complain, "Brother Barnett, would you recommend another church for me to pastor? My church won't do anything to win the lost." My response to letters like that is, "It's your job to provoke them to do something." That is what leadership is all about. You are as good a leader as you are a provoker of those around you.

PROVOKING FAMILIES TO ADVENTURE

Every summer growing up in Kansas City, my parents

would put me on a train—the Rock Island Zephyr—and tell the conductor not to let me off until I arrived in Bowie, Texas. I felt like such a grown-up, traveling all by myself. Once the train arrived at my destination, my grandparents would pick me up. The rest of the summer was spent having great adventures on the grounds of the Wagner Ranch, one of the largest ranches in the world, where my grandfather worked as a pumper for an oil company.

Our lone house was surrounded by rolling fields, thick foliage, wild horses, rattlesnakes, coyotes and wild game. I thought I was in paradise! Every day was a new adventure as I explored the vast open country. At the end of the summer, my grandparents would put me on the Rock Island Zephyr and send me back to Kansas City. Allowing me to travel all by myself was one way my parents instilled within me an appetite for adventure.

When I was young, my dad told me spellbinding stories of his travels to Europe as a young man. His inspiring anecdotes provoked me to follow in his footsteps and create adventures of my own. Then when I turned twenty-one, I embarked on my own trip around the world.

My parents exposed me not only to exciting adventures, but to great adventurers as well. The first Voice of Healing conference in 1950 was held in my father's church. As a child I sat on the laps of great healing evangelists like William Branham and Jack Coe, who stayed in our home. Men such as Oral Roberts and Gordon Lindsey were contemporaries of my father. They were daring, reckless, giant risk-takers who were adventurers in the faith. Observing these great men of God provoked me to follow in their footsteps and do great things for God as well. My dad was like those great men, and he created in me a thirst for adventure. My heroes were not movie stars or sports figures but preachers of the gospel.

Sufficiently provoked by my parents, Marja and I planned adventures for our children when they still lived at home so they could experience life to the fullest. One year I brought my children with me to Australia where I was speaking. There they saw great crowds, visited the outback and watched the kangaroos bobbing up and down the countryside. Exploring new places has a way of taking the blinders off children's eyes and exposing them to an exciting, new world that lies before them.

Another year my wife and daughter didn't want to take a vacation, so I took my boys to New York City where we visited the sites. As I mentioned earlier, we drove to inner-city Brooklyn where my sons played basketball with guys who really knew how to play.

Every day we went to Yankee Stadium to watch the Yankees. Coming home from a ball game one night, we boarded the subway along with a Brazilian father and son we had befriended at the game. After we were seated, three young men in leather jackets boarded our car and sat down fairly close to us. I wouldn't have noticed them except they were pretty rough-looking guys. While riding to our station, one of my boys overheard them saying, "We'll get 'em when they get off the subway."

My son turned to me and said, "Dad, they're gonna rob us!" I whispered to my Brazilian friends, "Stick close to us, and do what we do."

"OK," they replied.

When we arrived at our terminal, we stepped off the subway and hesitated for a moment, pretending to look at our map. Seeing that we were getting off, the three thieves stepped off the subway as well and nonchalantly proceeded around the corner where they waited for us. Looking at my map I reminded our group, "Now stick with me, and do what I do."

Just before the doors of the train closed, I said, "Jump back on!" We jumped back on the subway car, the doors closed and the guys ran out from behind the corner yelling at us. It was a good thing the windows were closed so we couldn't hear what they were saying. Experiences such as these exist, not only as exciting memories, but as provokers to adventure as well.

My run through the desert provoked Marja to become a long distance runner. She has run in the Los Angeles Marathon and has set a goal to run in all the major American marathons.

Growing up, my children were exposed to the adventure of ministry just as I was with my parents. My two sons and one daughter each worked their own bus route on Saturday mornings in some of the roughest areas of Phoenix. When my daughter was thirteen, she went door to door with a friend and invited people to church. Today, all of my children love God, they love the work of God and they love hurting people. Marja and I whetted their appetites for experiencing God's adventures by exposing them to people's needs.

THE FAMILY: A FIELD FOR PROVOKING

As I reflect upon the different men and women who provoked me in life, I would have to say that my parents were the biggest influence on me. God has ordained the family to be a field of provoking. Parents plant the seeds of the adventure of serving Jesus Christ into the lives of their children. They nurture and cultivate those seeds by exposing them to godly people, exciting family adventures and the presence of God. But in the end, it is God who gives the increase.

All too often, however, parents shield their children from the least bit of danger when they should be provoking them forward into adventure. Of course, there are boundaries. However, the natural impulse is to place safety over goodness rather than goodness over safety.

The problem with raising safe kids is that it runs in opposition to the Great Commission to go into all the world and preach the gospel to every creature. People who are afraid to have adventures become people who are afraid to share the gospel.

Parents need to learn the art of provoking their children—to care more than they have cared before, to work harder than they have worked before, to be more responsible than they have been before, to love Jesus more than they have before.

Parents in our Phoenix church have caught the vision of provoking spiritual adventure in the lives of their children. Today, our church lives for Los Angeles. Almost every week parents from our church send their teenagers to the Dream Center. Our youth are being changed as they are provoked to move beyond themselves and share Christ at the point of human need.

People from around the world as well are coming to help at the Dream Center. They aren't looking for safety—they are looking for an adventure.

ADVENTURE YOURSELF

THE VICARIOUS ADVENTURE

One of the great frustrations of any adventurer is the impossibility of enjoying more than one adventure at a time. I could put a bumper sticker on the back of my car that reads: "So many adventures, so little time."

Do you ever wish you could be in two places at once? Well, the joy that comes from provoking people to adventure lets you do just that. I call it *vicarious living*. In its true form, it is the most noble and gratifying kind of living.

Living vicariously means to experience the feelings of another person. When your little girl comes walking through the front door with her first report card in her hand, and you see what high marks she made, you can't help but feel a little bit of vicarious satisfaction. You almost feel as if you'd earned those As yourself. If you helped her with her homework, you probably did!

Paul's instruction in Romans 12:15 to "rejoice with those who rejoice, and weep with those who weep" is a scriptural example of vicarious living. As we experience vicariously the feelings of those around us, we can better minister to their needs and share the love of Jesus Christ.

Turning forty was an important juncture in my life. I had invitations from all over the world to preach revivals. God was blessing my ministry. But I asked myself, *Is this how I want to spend the rest of my life—traveling as an evangelist? What is the best way to win lost souls for Christ?* I concluded that I could make the greatest difference in my world and *the* world if I were to build a great soulwinning church—a church that would serve as a model of good works, provoking other churches to do the same.

God blessed our work in Davenport. Soon pastors were

asking me to help them in their work, so I began holding an annual Pastors' School, which now is in its twenty-third year. At the three-day school my pastoral staff and I share everything we know that will help people become better pastors and church leaders.

Today all over the country, pastors are preaching illustrated sermons, presenting pageants and operating bus ministries. I see the Pastors' School as one way of multiplying my work around the world. When reports come back to my office telling me how God used one of our ideas to win the lost for Christ, I experience the thrill of a vicarious adventure. A sense of satisfaction overwhelms me to know that somewhere in the world, men and women are reaching the lost for Christ, and in some sense, I am right there with them.

Through our Pastors College and Master's Commission, I have yet another opportunity to live the vicarious adventure and experience the fruit of another person's labors. But you don't have to have a Pastors' School or Master's Commission to make a difference. You have the opportunity to live vicariously through every person you touch for the kingdom.

I nurtured the seeds of planting a church in New York City in my heart even when their fulfillment seemed impossible. Years later, upon announcing to my church in Davenport that I had accepted the call to pastor in Phoenix, our children's pastor asked to meet with me.

"Pastor Barnett," he shared, "I know you've dreamed about going to New York City. But now with you leaving for Phoenix, perhaps for the rest of your life, your dream may never be fulfilled—by you. As you leave for Phoenix, I'll go to New York City, and you can live vicariously through me." Today I enjoy living the adventure through Bill Wilson, who is doing a great work with inner-city children in New York City.

By raising up my two sons to love God, I now live vicariously through them. Matthew pastors the Los Angeles International Church, which is currently one of the largest Assemblies of God church. And Luke pastors one of America's fastest-growing churches in Dayton, Ohio.

Larry Kerychuk, who has the ministry *Athletes in Ministry,* reaches world-class athletes with the gospel. Men such as Bill McCartney, Barry Sanders, Deion Sanders and David Robinson have all been impacted by his ministry. So in a sense, as I provoke Larry onward in the call God has on his life, I also live vicariously through him.

I hope that, as long as I live, God puts people in my life who provoke me to greater challenges. You too should be provoking people and surrounding yourself with people who provoke you so that your life and ministry don't become stale. Let us provoke one another–in the Lord!

EIGHTEEN

The Adventure of Living in Miracle Territory

What you can do or dream, begin it. Boldness has genius, power and magic in it.

—JOHANN WOLFGANG VON GOETHE

IN THE MIDST of working on this book, I flew to Australia for a series of meetings and then stopped in Los Angeles on my way back to Phoenix. Upon entering the Dream Center, I was greeted by my son Matthew. His face was ashen white, and he looked as if he had seen a ghost. Then he explained the reason for his appearance: "Dad, you won't believe what just happened. I have witnessed the greatest miracle of my life."

Late one night there was a lady walking around the parking lot with her daughter at the Dream Center. A volunteer approached the middle-aged woman and her thirteen-year-old disabled daughter. "We have come to live at the Dream Center. Aren't you open twenty-four hours a day?" she began. "We're homeless, and we need a place to stay for the night. I saw Matthew Barnett on television talking about the Dream Center, and immediately I knew we needed to live there. I would wait until tomorrow to work out all the details, but it's late and we don't have any money for a motel. We spent everything we had to get here. Could we please spend the night here with you?"

Although she could empathize with the plight of this poor woman and her daughter, the volunteer answered, "I'm sorry, but you'll have to come back tomorrow."

Running such an enormous operation and dealing with all kinds of people, we must run a tight ship. We have learned from experience that allowing people onto the premises late at night only invites trouble. Thus, we established a very strict policy stating that after 10:00 P.M., no one enters the Dream Center. No one.

"But I don't have a place to go," the mother pleaded.

"I'm sorry," the volunteer confessed, "but it is the Dream Center policy that no one can come in after 10:00 P.M. However, because we don't want to see anything bad happen to you tonight, we'll pay for you to stay at a motel nearby."

"Thank you," the mother replied, "but can my daughter at least use the restroom before we leave?" Bending the rules, the volunteer relented and allowed the woman and her daughter inside. The mentally disabled girl used the facilities while her mother and the supervisor remained outside in the hallway.

Suddenly, loud noises started coming from the restroom. The volunteer kicked the door in to find an open window and the girl hanging partially out the window. She was clinging desperately to the window frame. Somehow, the girl had crawled out the open window and was dangling six stories above the ground. Running to the window, the mother cried out, "Hold on!" She reached through the window, grabbing the girl's arm. While the volunteer ran to get help, the mother alternately tried hoisting her daughter back through the window and gently coaxing her to hang on.

Losing hope and strength, the girl finally let go and fell six stories to the ground below. With the sound of a sickening thud, the mother knew her daughter was dead. Peering through the bathroom window, she saw what appeared to be her daughter's lifeless body. But then the girl began to twitch and then move. Then she began to cry. Running down the hallway and six flights of stairs, the stunned mother rushed out onto the grassy area below and held her weeping daughter. Somehow, a three-foot-high bush that the girl had landed on broke her fall. Miraculously, the only injuries the girl sustained were a tiny crack in her elbow and a slightly split lip.

When Matthew shared the story, I was reminded of Eutychus in Acts 20. Sitting in the window sill while Paul preached into the night, he drifted into a deep sleep and fell out the window and onto the ground three stories below. The men brought Eutychus's body to Paul, who exclaimed (something like), "Don't worry, he's alive!" With that, the man came back to life. This was one of the greatest miracles of Paul's life. Most certainly, this was the greatest miracle of ours!

Looking back over the circumstances, I am convinced this was an all-out attempt by the devil to destroy the Dream Center.

But we are grateful to God for the miracle of saving this

girl's life. For a revival like we are experiencing to continue, we need miracles just to exist. And every step of the way we have seen them. Sometimes God waits until the last minute, but we're never short on miracles.

Some people ask me, "Why do miracles happen to you when they never happen to me?" My reply? *Because we live in miracle territory.*

FOUR KEYS TO BEING A MIRACLE

Not long ago, a man visited the church, and in an effort to compliment me, extolled, "Brother Barnett, you have literally performed miracles here. You're a miracle worker!" Immediately, I answered, "No, no, no. I have not performed any kind of a miracle, but I *am* a miracle."

The Bible tells us that we are the workmanship of God, created in Christ Jesus for good works (Eph. 2:10). No one is a miracle worker, but we can *be* miracles because it is God who works miracles in us!

In order to be a miracle, you don't have to have talent, charisma, ability or education. Just follow these four keys.

Key #1: Never pray for your tasks to equal your strength. Pray for strength to equal your tasks.

All too often we only want responsibilities commensurate with our abilities—the talent, resources and spiritual power we have at hand. But what distinguishes an adventure from normal living is that an adventure pushes people beyond the limits of their abilities.

God chose Gideon to be a miracle for the children of Israel. When informed of God's plan to use him, Gideon responded, "O my Lord, how can I save Israel? Indeed my clan is the weakest in Manasseh, and I am the least in my father's house" (Judg. 6:15). Gideon was looking for a task commensurate with his abilities. Had God worked a miracle according to Gideon's abilities, Israel would have never been delivered from the hands of the Midianites.

The area between the task and our ability to accomplish it is what I call *miracle territory*. That is the room we give God to work a miracle. I like to tell people, "Miracles take place in miracle territory." It is the playground of the adventurer. What Mt. Everest is to a mountain climber, miracle territory is to the spiritual adventurer.

The reason most people do not become miracles is that they do not give God any miracle territory. By living within their abilities, they give God little opportunity to intervene. That is why we need to be dangerous. Unless we venture out and take risks, we have little need for the power of God.

Gideon was poised for a God-sized adventure because he was living in miracle territory. He knew the task exceeded his ability, and the only way little old backwoods Gideon could defeat the armies of Midian would be if God performed a miracle. But if God could use Gideon to defeat the innumerable Midianite army, it would be one of the greatest adventures of all time.

When we survey the enormity of the task against the power we have to accomplish it, we should be able to say honestly, "I can't do all of that." And it's true—we can't. But if we add "except through Christ," then we *can* do all of it, as we say with the apostle Paul, "I can do all things *through Christ* who strengthens me" (Phil. 4:13, emphasis added).

ADVENTURE YOURSELF

By facing challenges that exceed our abilities, we are giving God a chance to act. But if we pare back our tasks, we are robbing ourselves of the opportunity to be miracles.

God is a miracle-working God. He can give us the strength to do what we are supposed to do, but we have to give Him the miracle territory that lies between the task and our ability.

When I met Dale Lane in Davenport, he was very shy and introverted. Speaking before groups of people made him stammer and stutter. One day he was asked to fill in for a bus pastor who wasn't able to lead a particular route that week. Although he felt inadequate, Dale agreed and did an excellent job. The next week the bus pastor again couldn't be there, so Dale again directed the same route, inviting people to church on Saturday and driving them to church on Sunday.

Dale grew into his job as a bus pastor. In fact, he became so good at it that he became a sectional bus director. When I moved to Phoenix he came with me to direct our bus ministry. Since then he has built one of the largest bus ministries in America. Today he holds the second highest office in our Phoenix church, that of executive pastor.

Dale is a prime example of a person who ventured out into miracle territory. He met an adventure that exceeded his ability. And because he took that step of faith, God made his ability commensurate with the adventure. That, my friend, is the way you become a miracle.

Key #2: Realize the task and your abilities never remain the same.

When our tasks are weighed against the power and strength we need, we usually find that our tasks exceed our power. We don't know how we can get everything accomplished in such little time. We fail to see how we can maintain our standard of living if we give more into the ministry of our church.

So, what do we do? Usually we chop off part of the task and move away from miracle territory. We only accomplish what our time schedule permits. Rather than giving sacrificially, we give according to our ability. I have found that when we chop off part of the task, God gives us less strength, and our power again fails to equal the task. Then when we meet another adventure that outweighs our ability, we chop off more of the adventure, leaving us with even less ability. The law of diminishing returns then goes to work against us, and we discover that we never have the power to equal the task.

In Jesus' parable of the talents in Matthew 25, a wealthy man went on a journey and entrusted one of his servants with five talents (one talent was roughly equivalent to fifteen years' wages), another servant with two talents and still another servant with one. The first two men used their talents and were rewarded with greater wealth and responsibilities. The one servant who did nothing with his *lost* what he had. When given greater responsibilities, he did nothing, and even what he had was taken away.

I know people gifted in ministry—musicians and preachers—who walked away from their God-given responsibilities. When they decided to return, they discovered their gifts weren't what they had been before. The anointing on their ministries was gone. The same is true of any adventure God calls you to accomplish.

On the other hand, have you ever noticed that the great men and women of God are busy people? Rather than turn down opportunities for ministry, they carry an ever-increasing load of responsibilities. People say, "If you want a job done, get a busy person to do it." It's true. You see, if you keep cutting down your tasks, God lessens your strength. But if you want to increase your tasks, your strength will increase, too.

Key #3: Begin the task before you have the strength.

When you walk into a gym, you notice weightlifters wincing under the weight they are lifting. The mantra of every serious athlete is, *No pain, no gain.*

Obviously weightlifters begin lifting a weight before they have the strength to lift it. At first, the weight seems heavy, but after numerous repetitions, day after day, the weight seems lighter. When the goal for lifting that particular weight is accomplished, the weightlifter then graduates to a heavier weight.

The point is that you do not get strength *for* the work, you get strength *from* the work. Every time you add more, God gives you more. If you are faithful in a few things, God gives you greater things. God doesn't give you strength for the burden—you get strength from the burden! The Bible promises:

> No temptation has overtaken you except such as is common to man; but God is faithful, who will not allow you to be tempted beyond what you are able, but with the temptation will also make the way of escape, that you may be able to bear it.
> —1 CORINTHIANS 10:13

When I face a task that exceeds my strength, I pray, "God, don't cut my work, because I know that You won't allow me to face more than what I can bear. If my task is larger, my strength will increase with it. I want to grow, God, so make my responsibilities greater."

But some say, "Pastor, I have so much on my plate, I just can't do any more." I have always had more than I can handle, but God has always reassured me, "You do it, and I will give you strength while you do it. You can't afford it, but when you perform the ministry, the money will follow the ministry."

Without our living in miracle territory, the Dream Center would have never come into existence. Naysayers will always question the viability of every adventure we pursue. Yet more miracles have resulted from this work than from any other ministry with which I have been associated. But in order to experience the miracle, we had to venture into miracle territory.

Key #4: Never pray to do *miracles, but to* be *one.*

Every person needs to find out once and for all if there is a God in heaven or not. Will He give you power to perform the task He has given you or not? You won't be a miracle by waiting while the right opportunity passes you by. You are not going to be a miracle by saying you can't do it.

The only way that you can be a miracle is if you live in miracle territory, if you perform the task you thought you were incapable of performing. Don't wait for all the details to come together—just do it! Ask God for a God-sized adventure.

Why don't you try something big? Why don't you just say, "I serve a God who gives power equal to the task. God is the miracle worker. I'm just the work."

There once was a little Indian boy dying of tuberculosis. The doctor gave him no hope to live. He was skin and bones, but a miracle healed that little boy, and he went on to build Oral Roberts University.

There was a little illegitimate child whose mother did not want him, so she turned him over to a minister. He felt unloved, but that little boy grew up to become James Robison, one of America's great evangelists.

Gideon realized he was living in miracle territory, so he decided to venture forward and mobilize the troops of Israel. God told Gideon to reduce the number of troops from thirty-two thousand men to a manageable three hundred men. With such a disparity between the legions of Midianite troops and Israel's diminutive army, adequate miracle territory was established for God to intervene. Because Gideon refused to pare down the task, God gave Gideon the victory over the Midianites, who vastly outnumbered the troops of Israel.

Gideon was no different from you or me. He grew up in an insignificant family from one of the weakest tribes of Israel. But he believed God and stepped into a situation that only God could bail him out of. He stepped into miracle territory, where the miracles occur.

NINETEEN

The Adventure Is Worth It All

Some men see things as they are and ask why. I dream things that never were and say, why not?

—GEORGE BERNARD SHAW

THE LOS ANGELES SUN shone down on us in the parking lot of the Dream Center. Soft winds blew in from the Pacific Ocean, and the day seemed to enfold us with its goodwill. The Hollywood sign was visible from where we stood, and I could hear the freeways in the distance bustling with traffic. I could faintly remember the sound of gunshots, so common when we first took the Dream Center, but now much less so. It all seemed so perfect, this inner-city wedding at a place where so many dreams had been born. I couldn't have been happier as I stood on the platform and watched Matthew come down the aisle—the groom about to embark on one of

207

life's greatest adventures, marriage.

Three thousand people, rich and poor, had joined us for the most adventurous wedding I had ever attended. Behind me stood the pastors of three of America's largest churches. On the front row sat Kevin Malone, general manager of the Los Angeles Dodgers and Matthew's friend. Also there were Lou Rawls, who sang during the ceremony, and actress Dyan Cannon, one of Hollywood's most wonderful Christian ladies.

Three buses had gone into Los Angeles to pick up people from skid row, where the homeless lived in boxes. Buses rolled down Sunset Boulevard to gather up the kids with blue and pink hair, nose rings and tattoos. The diverse crowd reminded me of the wedding feast in the Bible with the lame, the halt and the blind.

Many were there who had been helped by a feeding program created by Matthew's bride, a beautiful Swedish girl named Caroline. One day, Caroline had gone to Matthew and said she wanted to start a feeding program. "We have no food," my son replied. Undeterred, Caroline went to the U.S. Department of Agriculture and struck a deal with them: If they gave her food, she would keep a complete list of where the food had gone so they would know it wasn't wasted. Every day, this slight woman and three other ladies loaded up a truck with fifty-pound boxes and took it to the streets where they shared the gospel of Christ. On Sunday, they picked those same people up for church.

On her wedding day, many of the people Caroline had fed over the past year were there. Fifty kids from the Dream Center elementary school, wearing beautiful white robes, ran down the aisle in front of the bride, ringing bells and announcing her entrance.

Then, in the crowd, I saw Gena, an eighteen-year-old girl who once worked the streets as a prostitute. One night she was turning tricks when a man picked her up and took her down an alley to transact some business. Placing a knife against her throat, he told her, "If you scream, I'm gonna cut your throat and you'll die." The experience scared her to death. Having been a prostitute for only three weeks, she realized that if she were to continue down that path, it could very well cost her life.

Three o'clock the following morning, workers from our ministry to prostitutes gave her a flower as they always do to women of the night and told her that Jesus loved her. That act of kindness broke through her hurting heart, and she expressed interest in moving into the Dream Center.

In a scene reminiscent of the television show *Mission Impossible,* our people organized a getaway for Gena. As they pulled up next to her on the street and she hopped into the car, her pimp, not wanting to lose his investment, pursued from behind in his car. When our workers pulled into the Dream Center parking lot, the pimp gave up his pursuit and returned to the streets.

Since then Gena has given her life to the Lord, and today she has graduated from our discipleship program. As I looked at her face, it was obvious that her innocence had been restored.

I looked out again and saw Billy Soto who, as I mentioned earlier in the book, played guitar in a rock-and-roll band for thirty years. His addiction to heroin cost him his wife and his family. But today, Billy lives for Jesus Christ and has been reunited with his wife and family. Working with people living under the bridges and people with AIDS, he has become a vital part of our ministry.

Then I saw a man we call "Earthquake" Kelley. A heavy-weight boxer, about 6 feet 5 inches tall and 275 pounds, he looks like an earthquake waiting to happen. He had given his life to Christ decades earlier, and is now on our staff working with gang members and teaching classes on boxing and self-defense.

On December 7, 1998, his two sons were driving home from work when they stopped at a stoplight. A thug ran up to their window, put a gun to his twenty-six-year-old son's head and shouted, "I want your car." The young man stepped out of the car, but as the carjacker got in, he pulled the trigger and killed the young man on the spot. His son gave his life to save his brother's.

When Earthquake Kelley heard the news of his son's death, he was devastated. I called him from Phoenix, and Earthquake confessed to me, "Pastor, I don't understand it. I've given my life to help these people, and this is what I get in return. I used to be a gang member, and it wouldn't be that hard to take revenge on the man who robbed my son of his life."

As we continued talking, his anger turned from wanting to exact revenge to wanting to walk away from his gang ministry. Then he asked, "Is it wrong to feel that way?"

"No," I responded. "Earthquake, I understand and God understands. You have a right to feel that way."

We flew him out to Phoenix so I could spend some extended time with Earthquake and his other son. Later, he called me on the phone. "Pastor Barnett, I want to apologize for my actions the other day. I've decided that if God was willing to give His Son to save the world, then I'll give my son and use his death to win more people to Jesus Christ." Today he works with young men just like the ones who took his son's life.

Seeing Earthquake Kelley lifted my spirits even higher.

Then I saw Willette Brown whom we met through our bus ministry. When she first came to the Dream Center she was skin and bones as a result of crack habit. One of her sons had been shot and killed by a young man who wanted his tennis shoes. Her other children had been taken away from her because of her drug problem.

Willette came to our church services and gave her life to Christ, but she still struggled with returning to her old lifestyle. Her husband, James, forced drugs on her. Finally, one of the ladies in our church said, "I'm taking you to live at the Dream Center." Practically forcing her to pack her bags, the woman brought Willette to us. Living on the premises, Willette grew healthy and strong.

Six months later her husband called me and said, "Look, I need a change. Would you let me stay at the Dream Center, too?"

I thought to myself, *He doesn't mean it. He just wants to drag his wife down with him.* I really didn't want him to come, so I figured I would make it hard for him.

"OK," I answered, "you can come to live at the Dream Center, but first you'll need to live out at the ranch for ninety days." The ranch is an intensive discipleship school outside the L.A. city limits where we normally keep people for thirty days. I figured that if he was really serious, he'd be able to last ninety days. He went to the ranch and graduated with flying colors. James cleaned up his act, got his life right with God, and today he's the head of our discipleship program.

Seeing Willette reach over to take her husband by the hand made my eyes well up with tears. Even her children had been given back to her. Something inside me said, *We've made a difference. We've made a difference.*

As the emotional and joyful service continued, I held up two mementoes, one a blanket of Caroline's from when she was a child, the other a trophy Matthew had won wrestling. People were crying all over the place as I spoke about my son and soon-to-be daughter-in-law. All I could think, standing there with all those marvelous folks, was, *It pays to be in the most exciting adventure of all: the adventure of others.*

The adventure of serving Jesus Christ surpasses the adventure any explorer or extreme athlete has—period. It knits people together in a supernatural way. Man's adventures don't even compare to God's.

I hope by now you understand that you can embark on your own adventure with God:

- Working in the inner city
- Venturing out onto the mission field
- Building a great church and winning a city for God
- Starting a dream center of your own in your city
- Making a difference in your world

Whatever it is you do, my prayer is that you will be satisfied with nothing less than God's adventure for your life. Forsake small dreams and pursue God's dreams.

Adventure yourself!

Notes

INTRODUCTION
AN APPETITE FOR ADVENTURE

1. Internet source: Fox TV Web Site: www.fox.com/frameset.html.
2. Gregg Zoroya, "I Spy," *USA Today,* 15 October 1999.

CHAPTER ONE
DREAMS DELAYED COME TRUE

1. Michael P. Green, *Illustrations for Biblical Preaching* (Grand Rapids, MI: Baker Book House, 1989). From Bible Illustrator for Windows software, version 3.0c, Hiawatha, IA: Parson's Technology.

CHAPTER FIVE
THE HEART OF THE ADVENTURE

1. *Life and Times Tonight,* December 25, 1998. Produced by KCET, Los Angeles.

CHAPTER SEVEN
THE ADVENTURE OF GIVING ALL

1. Craig Brian Larson, "Strong to the Finish," *Preaching Today,* Tape No. 155. From Bible Illustrator for Windows software, version 3.0c, Hiawatha, IA: Parson's Technology.
2. "I Surrender All" by Judson Van DeVenter. Public domain.

CHAPTER EIGHT
THE ADVENTURE OF TAKING RISKS

1. Compiled by Lisa Tabb with additional reporting by Peter Heller and Lisa Jones; "Trips 2000: The 25 Greatest Adventures in the World," *National Geographic*

Magazine, Fall 1999, 74–95.

2. These seven points are from a tape by Dr. Mark Rutland.

3. Quoted in *Marriage Partnership,* Vol. 7, no. 3. Bible Illustrator version 3.0c, Parsons Technology.

CHAPTER NINE
THE ADVENTURE OF FACING YOUR FEARS

1. James S. Hewett, *Illustrations Unlimited* (Wheaton: Tyndale House Publishers, 1988), 130.

2. H. V. Synan, *Dictionary of Pentecostal and Charismatic Movements* (Grand Rapids, MI: Zondervan, 1988).

CHAPTER ELEVEN
THE ADVENTURE OF FAITHFULNESS

1. Johannes Du Plessis, *The Life of Andrew Murray in South Africa* (London: Marshall Brothers, Ltd, 1919), 197.

CHAPTER TWELVE
THE ADVENTURE OF OTHERS

1. Michael P. Green, *Illustrations for Biblical Preaching* (Grand Rapids, MI: Baker Book House, 1989). From Bible Illustrator for Windows software, version 3.0c, Hiawatha, IA: Parson's Technology.

CHAPTER THIRTEEN
THE ADVENTURE OF GIVING

1. Scott Kirsner, "Non-profit Motive," *Wired Magazine,* September 1999.

CHAPTER FOURTEEN
THE ADVENTURE OF LIVING BEYOND SAFE

1. Beth Prim Howell, *Lady on a Donkey* (New York: E. P. Dutton & Co., 1960); and Lester F. Sumrall *Lillian*

Trasher, the Nile Mother (Springfield, MO: Gospel Publishing House, 1951).
2. C. S. Lewis, *The Lion, the Witch, and the Wardrobe* (New York: HarperCollins, 1950), 80.
3. Bill Wundram, "Here's-s-s-s Tommy!" *Quad-CityTimes*, August 18, 1992, p. 02A.

CHAPTER FIFTEEN
THE ADVENTURE OF WANTING TO QUIT

1. Steve Blankenship, *Leadership*, Vol. 6, no. 1. From Bible Illustrator for Windows software, version 3.0c, Hiawatha, IA: Parson's Technology.

CHAPTER SIXTEEN
THE ADVENTURE OF GOING A LITTLE FARTHER

1. John C. Maxwell, *Leadership 101: Inspirational Quotes & Insights for Leaders,* (Tulsa, OK: Honor Books, 1989), 59.

CHAPTER NINETEEN
THE ANTIDOTE TO BURNOUT

1. Army Archerd, "Just for Variety," *Daily Variety,* May 19, 1998, p. 4.

You can experience more of God's grace & love!

If you would like free information on how you can know God more deeply and experience His grace, love and power more fully in your life, simply write or e-mail us. We'll be delighted to send you information that will be a blessing to you.

To check out other titles from **Creation House** that will impact your life, be sure to visit your local Christian bookstore, or call this toll-free number:

1-800-599-5750

For free information from Creation House:

CREATION HOUSE
600 Rinehart Rd.
Lake Mary, FL 32746
www.creationhouse.com

Your Walk With God Can Be Even Deeper...

With *Charisma* magazine, you'll be informed and inspired by the features and stories about what the Holy Spirit is doing in the lives of believers today.

Each issue:
- Brings you exclusive world-wide reports to rejoice over.
- Keeps you informed on the latest news from a Christian perspective.
- Includes miracle-filled testimonies to build your faith.
- Gives you access to relevant teaching and exhortation from the most respected Christian leaders of our day.

Call 1-800-829-3346 for 3 FREE trial issues
Offer #AOACHB

If you like what you see, then pay the invoice of $22.97 (**saving over 51% off the cover price**) and receive 9 more issues (12 in all). Otherwise, write "cancel" on the invoice, return it, and owe nothing.

Experience the Power of Spirit-Led Living

Charisma Offer #AOACHB
P.O. Box 420234
Palm Coast, Florida 32142-0234
www.charismamag.com